THE
GREAT
COLLECTORS

THE GREAT COLLECTORS

Masterpieces From Private Collections

by Véronique Prat

Translated by Michael Edwards

TABARD PRESS

Tabard Press
27 West 20th Street
New York, N.Y. 10011

Copyright © 1988 Editions Albin Michel, Paris

English translation © 1990 William S. Konecky Associates, Inc.

Translated by Michael Edwards.

ISBN: 0-914427-38-5

Printed and bound in Hong Kong

Contents

A Journalistic
Coup

"I spend three hundred million francs a year purchasing works of art . . . As much as the Metropolitan Museum in New York. And more than most of the great museums of Europe."

Neither boastful nor bashful, Heinrich Thyssen is simply stating the facts. It is true that Thyssen's twelve hundred paintings can hold their own with the most famous public collections. But his collection—like those of Armand Hammer, Akram Ojjeh, Prince von Fürstenberg, the Duchess of Alba, Walter Annenberg, and a good many others—is different. They are private collections, jealously guarded by their owners; theirs are secret masterpieces.

Consequently, *Figaro Magazine* found it a tempting notion to flush some of these collections out into the open, to give the public its first view of them through the most beautiful reproductions that the French press could offer. A journalistic coup of international scope, and an intriguing introduction to a group of remarkable individuals . . .

"If you can be in Los Angeles next Monday, Mr. Hammer will be happy to see you. He will be arriving from London at 10 A.M. and will not be leaving for Moscow till late afternoon."

This is a typical example of what it is like to get hold of these people: traveling an obstacle course that zigzags between Tokyo, New York, Amsterdam, and Zurich. So when do they get to enjoy their beautiful homes, these men and women who spend more time in the air than on the ground? Now, there's an idea . . . I immediately call back Armand Hammer's secretary: "What if I meet up with Mr. Hammer in London? Could I interview him during the flight?"

OK. So it is in his private Boeing, at thirty thousand feet, that "Doc" Hammer tells me how he, a poor kid from the Bronx, became a billionaire; how he managed to swipe a Rembrandt from under the nose of the fabulously wealthy Getty Museum; how, because the demands of his business prevented him from going to London, he bought a Michelangelo by phone (!); why one day he offered Brezhnev a Goya. When we arrive in Los Angeles, Hammer politely asks if I can give him an hour to freshen up before the photo session, and then, like a Hollywood star, he is adamant about being taken from his good side!

Another businessman whose activities are spread across three continents, Prince von Fürstenberg considers it a point of honor to make you forget that he is overwhelmed with work. Two weeks before the date set for our meeting, a letter bearing the prince's coat of arms ("or a bordure nebulé argent and azure, the field charged with an eagle gules, beaked and membered azure") informs me that I am expected at Donaueschingen Castle, the family estate, where the former chambers of Kaiser Wilhelm II have been prepared for me.

Alas, my arrival is not as elegant. When *Figaro Magazine* covers the great private collections, it means bringing along four hundred pounds of photographic gear, eight studio lights, a total of eighteen cases crammed with equipment. Driving up, we look like the Beverly Hillbillies, but Joachim von Fürstenberg seems not to notice a thing. In the hands of a half-dozen servants, the ragtag baggage miraculously disappears, and it is with dignity restored that I reach my chambers, which the Prince has brightened on this gray winter's day with roses by the dozen. For two days, he graciously allows himself to be photographed, shows me through his castle, recounts his ancestral history, and explains the origin of his fabulous collection with a dozen panels by Hans Holbein the Elder. No museum in the world can match it!

"Dear girl, what you are asking me is impossible. I never lend my paintings to exhibitions, so to allow them to be published in a newspaper—out of the question!"

The setting is no longer Germany in winter but Italy in springtime, and things seem to be starting off on the wrong foot. We are in Rome, in the music room of the Palazzo Pallavicini-Rospigliosi; Princess Pallavicini, the picture of elegance in her Givenchy suit, smiles at me, unwavering. My mind races: It's impossible, she can't be refusing me. This collection is superb, I just have to have it. But what to do? Give up? No. The sight of a *Virgin and Child* by Botticelli decides me. It *would* be a Botticelli; there are three of them here, in the only private collection that can boast such riches. In the room with us are the Princess's private secretary and her confessor (a marvelously intelligent and cultured French priest); at the moment, we are talking about painting. My article is forgotten, eclipsed by the seventeenth-century struggle in Rome between the "Classicism" of the Carraccis and the "Realism" of Caravaggio. Suddenly, the Princess turns to me: "Go ahead! Write your story, you have my permission."

No one before had been given access to this collection. No one has had access to it since. An exclusive, a real scoop. And for me, it was more than a beautiful collection; it was the chance to meet a great lady.

Never have I traveled so far from France to see French paintings. Halfway round the world: a plane to Tokyo, then the "bullet" train to Kurashiki, on the southeast coast of Honshu—all to see Monet, Degas, Renoir . . . Here the people still wear traditional dress, kimonos in shimmering silks. It is like traveling back in time. So much so that on the station platform, our modern little group creates a sensation. A man, jovial and smiling, pushes through the crowd. A deep bow: "I am Kenichiro Oohara." He takes us into the village and up to a big, beautiful wooden house, built in the eighteenth century: the home of a powerful family of industrialists and art lovers.

Kenichiro asks me to remove my shoes and gestures toward a rectangular cushion placed on the floor: "Please be seated." I had not been informed that being an art reporter required the asceticism of a Zen monk. For two hours, seated on the tatami, my legs tucked under me and my posture erect, I listened to Kenichiro Oohara tell me how his grandfather came to buy some Monet canvases in 1920, when contemporary Western art was completely unknown in Japan. It is fascinating, but I can't go on; my knees are aching and my spine has turned to jelly. Like a coward, I beseech Kenichiro to find us two armchairs for the rest of the interview. If I have lost face, so be it . . .

The collection is superb, and if today the Japanese are the principal buyers at the big international art auctions, outbidding even the Americans, it is all due to the pioneering Ooharas, who introduced Manet, Degas, Renoir, and their fellows to Japan.

In my honor, she is wearing a pink plastic watch! And in the photo, all you can see are her big blue eyes with their long lashes. No, we're not in Hollywood, visiting some showbiz art collector. We're in the English countryside, at Lady Jessica's.

To be more exact, at the home of her father, Lord Egremont, but Jessica, age seven, seems to be in charge of things. Immediately upon our arrival at the family manor, she shows us where to park, informs the gardener that we are from *Figaro Magazine* (which seems to arouse only mild interest in the old man), and announces that the day's first cup of tea will be served in the library in ten minutes. There I find Max Egremont (not yet forty) who casts a tender gaze on his eldest daughter. Quite simply, he adores children, and he would like to have a score of them, one for each Turner on his walls!

I counted five little Egremonts; but as for the Turners, I saw all twenty, distributed among the Turner Room, the Great Hall, and the vast corridor of the North Wing. It's impressive. Not even New York's Metropolitan Museum nor London's National Gallery nor Paris's Louvre can exhibit such an assortment.

While the photographers are busy setting up, Jessica is constantly at their heels. This will be my "homiest" story, marked by the feeding times of the youngest boy, the baby talk of frolicsome Lord George, age three, and not to mention my croquet match with Jessica. I gave it my all, but it was just her day . . .

Who would have imagined that something so fantastic would take place in such a quiet country? I had arranged to meet Peter Nathan in the residential quarter of Zurich. A serious man, this Nathan. In the microcosm of the art world, everyone knows his infallible eye, his encyclopedic knowledge, his perfect taste. Together, we had chosen from among his many Géricaults, Delacroixs, and Courbets those that would appear in our layout. All that remained was to photograph them. While we were making our choice, our ace art photographer, Peter Willi, had set up a makeshift studio in one of the rooms of the Nathan Gallery, situated some five hundred yards from the house of the great art dealer. To make the job easier, Nathan offered to supply the transportation. And so it was that the two of us set off through the streets of Zurich with the Courbets, Renoirs, and Géricaults tucked under our arms.

The scene had more than a touch of the surreal: two people calmly strolling through the streets of a city, loaded down with some of the most renowned (and expensive!) masterpieces of nineteenth-century French art. I had the impression that all the passers-by were looking at us. I was sure that any second someone was going to leap out of a doorway and snatch our precious cargo, as tempting as gold ingots. But Nathan seemed unworried. At most, he was amused by my panic. When the delivery was safely completed, I had a stiff drink—the one time, I assure you, that I have ever partaken while on duty.

My memories of these very famous or very retiring private collectors jostle against each other like crowds at a museum. The motorcycle rides with Malcolm Forbes "because paintings are nice, but you've got to do something physical." The rounds of golf on Walter Annenberg's private course—acres of manicured fairways in the middle of the Nevada desert, where Ronald Reagan escaped from the White House every New Year's, and where Queen Elizabeth has also hit some beautiful drives. Returning from the hunt with Prince von Hohenzollern, nature lover and one of the best shots in Europe.

Then there was Countess Harrach, who was sorry that our visit was in winter: "It is simply the worst season to see my garden!" Or Akram Ojjeh, who was in the midst of moving from one magnificent Parisian mansion to another and asked if we could postpone our story until the housewarming . . .

Certainly, some stories were not as "easy" as others, but I won't complain. Instead, I shall recall the words of Élie Faure: "Art is the call to the communion of man."

A Little Louvre
in L.A.

Six o'clock in the morning. The California sun kisses the Pacific, whitening the deserted beach in front of Norton Simon's Malibu home.

Shivering in his plaid swim trunks, Simon charges down from the deck and plunges into the ocean for his daily three-mile swim. Not an ounce of fat, 175 pounds of muscle. Pretty good for a septuagenarian! At the moment, he is floating on his back, revealing only his craggy face embellished with wrinkles, an aquiline nose, and a sorrowful, remarkably intelligent expression.

An hour later, wearing beige trousers and a light blue shirt, Simon is seated in his office. A big swivel chair in fawn-colored leather, a table strewn with catalogues and photos. His right hand firmly grasps his favorite tool, the telephone. Norton Simon—billionaire, head of one of the biggest consortiums in the United States, and world-renowned art collector—is hard at work.

"You blew it this time," he bellows at the cringing broker who failed to buy Texaco at the right price. His voice sometimes rises, sometimes drops to a whisper. But he is never asked to repeat himself. "You're always blowing it," Simon barks before hanging up. On line two, a gallery is calling from New York about a painting. Simon goes straight to the point:

"How much do you want for it? Three hundred and fifty?" (Thousand, of course.)

With his left hand, he plays endlessly with the coins in his pocket. Though it seems a quick decision, he has put a lot of thought into it, seen the work several times, and spent hours on the phone to New York, London, and Paris, seeking the opinions of specialists. Thus, by dint of intelligence and hard work, Norton Simon has taken less than twenty years to assemble one of the most spectacular art collections in existence. The proof: Raphael, El Greco, Memling, Cranach, Frans Hals, Murillo (two), Zurbaran (four), Rubens (also four), Rembrandt (three), Canaletto, Guardi (three), Watteau, Degas (twenty-one, not counting the pastels and sculptures), Manet (three), Cézanne (four), Renoir (six), Monet (four), Toulouse-Lautrec (three), Gauguin, van Gogh (five), Douanier Rousseau, Picasso (ten)! An extraordinary story, for an extraordinary man.

*Norton Simon beside one of the most illustrious paintings in
his collection: Rembrandt's Portrait of Titus. It has taken
Simon less than twenty years to assemble a collection valued
at over half a billion dollars!*

Like his collection, Simon's fortune was built from scratch. He was born in 1907 in Oregon. His father was a floorwalker in a Portland department store. Norton's childhood was anything but pampered, especially when the store's bankruptcy put his father in the unemployment line. Norton vowed to overcome it: the poverty, the run-down house, his mother worn out with housework, his father's threadbare suit. But in America in 1929, success was hardly guaranteed . . .

Norton, however, made his own "New Deal": In 1931, he invested his savings, seven thousand dollars, in a failing fruit-juice company. He worked furiously, bought up his partners' shares, modernized the bottling system, invested in a massive advertising campaign to launch his brand (Val Vita Foods) nationwide. Some years later, Simon knew he had succeeded. Sales had increased from $43,000 to $9,000,000!

What followed is classic Norton Simon. He set his sights on gaining control of his big rival, Hunt Brothers. He sold his company to Hunt and immediately reinvested by buying all Hunt shares available on the market. He had infiltrated the opposition camp; soon after, holding 25% of Hunt stock, he became chairman, and a successful one. Sales climbed rapidly and reached $100 million.

It was rags to riches. Lots of riches. And with the same mixture of assurance and nerve that brought him Hunt Foods, Simon took control of the Ohio Match Co., *McCall's*, Canada Dry, the Northern Pacific Railroad, Johnnie Walker Scotch—an empire that he modestly baptized "Norton Simon, Inc."

Like Rockefeller, Carnegie, Ford, and Morgan before him, Simon used his new fortune to acquire works of art. At first timidly—he spent hours looking at paintings at the Metropolitan Museum in New York and the National Gallery in Washington, D.C.; visited London, Paris, and Rome; met experts and museum curators; immersed himself in treatises on art history. At last he came to a decision: His first purchase was to be a Gauguin, soon followed by a Picasso—two paintings that he has since sold. They no longer met the "Norton Simon standard."

In 1969, in order to devote more time to his collection, Simon gave up the presidency of his company, becoming simply a consultant. There was panic in the New York business world, but he retorted simply: "I no longer enjoyed it."

What he now enjoys is contemplating the purchase of the very beautiful *Christ Blessing* by Hans Memling; outbidding the museums for the last Raphael painting still in private hands; musing before his Rembrandts, especially the *Portrait of Titus*, his first important purchase.

Jacopo Bassano

The Flight into Egypt (detail)
Oil on canvas, 46.9 × 88.0 in.; 119 × 198 cm.

After studying the rudiments of his art with his father, Bassano traveled in about 1540 to Venice, where he eagerly subscribed to the formulas then in fashion: slender, elegant figures; bright, acid colors. Later, his style evolved toward a realism similar to that of the seventeenth-century Spanish painters, whose taste for "lifelike" detail and violent lighting he shared.

The year was 1965. That day, Simon, not yet known as a collector, burst onto the art scene. In front of the curators of the principal museums of Europe and the United States, in front of art connoisseurs of international standing—Thyssen, Hammer, Niarchos—he alone would dare (perhaps he alone was able!) to pay $2,235,000 for a piece of canvas measuring 25 inches by 22 inches (but signed by Rembrandt!). A colossal sum at the time.

Like the eighth wonder of the world, the painting was shown in London, then Simon lent it for six months to the National Gallery in Washington and for a year to the Rijksmuseum in Amsterdam.

Since then, the Rembrandt has produced offspring. Today, the Simon Collection numbers close to five hundred paintings, dating from the fifteenth to the twentieth centuries. All the schools, all the great names are there, represented by major works. Some years ago, Norton married the actress Jennifer Jones (in a very romantic ceremony that took place at four in the morning aboard a friend's yacht in the middle of the English Channel). Since our meeting, they have moved from the immense house in Malibu to a Beverly Hills mansion. The result was a battle of wills. Jennifer, an orchid lover, wanted to have them throughout the house, while Norton protested that there wouldn't be any room for his paintings.

The solution? Norton has given Jennifer a magnificent arrangement of roses, peonies, and tulips.

Painted by Renoir.

Paul Gauguin

The Pink Dress
Oil on canvas, 37.4 × 24.4 in.; 95 × 62 cm.

Gauguin painted this work while in Tahiti for the second time. It was an unhappy sojourn. During the winter of 1898, he attempted suicide; in 1901, he sought to flee even farther, to the Marquesas. Yet Gauguin's paintings during these three years (The Pink Dress is from 1899) were the most relaxed, the most truly Tahitian of his career.

14

15

Hans Memling

Christ Blessing
Wood, 15.0 × 11.4 in.; 38 × 29 cm.

Rembrandt

Self-Portrait
Wood, 24.8 × 20.1 in.; 63 × 51 cm.

From fifteenth-century Flanders to seventeenth-century Holland there was a slow evolution from idealized, monumental art toward the study of the subject's psychology. On the one hand, Memling's serenity, and on the other, Rembrandt's lucid and realistic observation.

16

Edgar Degas

Dancer on Point

Gouache and pastel on paper,
21.7 × 29.1 in.; 55 × 74 cm.

In Degas's work there are several series: horse races, laundresses, women after the bath, the world of cafés and honky-tonks, and especially ballet dancers. They are all represented in the Simon Collection, of which this marvelous pastel, dating from 1877, is one of the highlights.

Henri de Toulouse-Lautrec

Red-Haired Woman in a Garden

Oil on cardboard, 28.0 × 20.5 in.;
71 × 52 cm.

With his taste for unusual composition, the expressive force of his drawing, and his exploration of sumptuous colors—intense reds and greens, mauve shadows—Lautrec was always a keen observer (and a kinder one than has been suggested), whose daring presaged the Fauves and Expressionists.

18

Henri Rousseau

Exotic Landscape

Oil on canvas, 51.2 × 64.2 in.;
130 × 163 cm.

Dating from 1910, the year of Rousseau's death, this canvas clearly shows his highly original, modern-Primitive style, guileless in its sensibility, but very deliberate in its technique, which gave birth to the twentieth-century current of "Naive" art.

20

The Lord with Four-and-Twenty Canalettos

A flock of goats! Unafraid, the little creatures gambol and bleat around our car, escorting us right up to the front door of the mansion with its beautiful eighteenth-century façade. One might wish for a more dignified introduction, but the master of the house, coming out onto the steps to meet me, is reassuring:

"At our house, the goats are "persona grata'; they have been on the family coat of arms for five centuries. These ones seem to have adopted you. Welcome."

Ten o'clock on a Monday morning at Woburn Abbey, the ancestral home of the Dukes of Bedford. The heir to the title, Lord Tavistock, invites us to join him for the day's first cup of tea. Jolly good idea, what? Woburn is very beautiful, but sprawling—one hundred and twenty rooms, over ten miles of walls, five hundred and sixty windows, ninety-seven telephones, eleven ghosts . . . And thousands of paintings: Rembrandt and van Dyck, Nicolas Poussin and Claude Lorrain, Frans Hals and Murillo, Reynolds and Gainsborough, and the spectacular series of twenty-four Canalettos, unequaled by any other private collection, even Queen Elizabeth II's. What, then, could cause Lord Tavistock to sigh?

"We've come a long way," he explains. "When my father succeeded to the title, in 1953, Woburn was terribly run down: holes in the roof, walls collapsing, sagging beams. The works of art were piled up any old how: the Rembrandts alongside the frying pans, the Vincennes porcelain pieces stacked among the chamber pots."

However, the thirteenth Duke of Bedford and his eldest son, Lord Tavistock, rescued it all. The collection is intact. Now Tavistock permits himself a smile. "I shall introduce you to those who created this collection. Come meet my ancestors."

Lord Tavistock leads me at a smart pace to Woburn's portrait gallery. He stops before a man with a white beard.

"Here is the first earl, a notorious smuggler. And the second, who was regarded as the ugliest man in all of Europe. Here you see the fifth; he was made a duke to console him over the death of his son, who was unjustly beheaded."

A few steps farther, on the left wall: "Here is the third duke. Thank God, he died young; otherwise his gambling would have ruined us all!"

Robin, Marquess of Tavistock and eldest son of the thirteenth Duke of Bedford, in the library of the family manor, Woburn Abbey. On the walls, an impressive series of self-portraits by Rembrandt, Hals, van Dyck, Murillo, Reynolds . . . In the dining room, the renowned series of twenty-four Canalettos.

Another few steps. Perhaps I'm only imagining it, but it seems to me that Lord Tavistock suddenly becomes pensive. We are before the portrait of the fourth duke, a man in a powdered wig, with a sturdy bearing, but a crafty expression, handsomely painted here by Thomas Gainsborough. Tavistock continues soberly:

"Here's John; he loved to travel, and managed a bit of shopping while he was at it."

Typical English understatement. He was the family's first great collector. Thanks to him, Woburn Abbey's breakfast room is commonly referred to as the "Reynolds Room," on account of the seven paintings by the greatest English portraitist that hang there. The library, decorated in the purest Regency style and one of the most fascinating rooms at Woburn, is home to three Rembrandts, a Frans Hals, a van Dyck, a Hogarth (probably the single existing self-portrait by the artist), a Murillo . . . And the dining room is called the "Canaletto Room" because twenty-four canvases by the eighteenth-century Italian master—nothing less than the most important grouping in the world—grace its walls. So much for the fourth duke's "shopping"!

In Rome and Venice, he acquired paintings (Carracci, Tintoretto, Poussin). In Paris, where he served as His Majesty's ambassador, he bought furniture bearing the stamp of Gaudreau, Riesener, and Langlois, and in 1763 received as a gift from Louis XV an extraordinary service of Sèvres porcelain. (All 183 pieces have survived to the present day!) Decorated with birds on a blue background, it is reserved for special occasions—Christmas Day, for instance, or when Queen Elizabeth drops in for tea. On those days, for good measure, the family silver is also brought out: goblets encrusted with gold coins, silver candelabra wrought by Jules-Robert Auguste, and grand vermeil trays.

Though patiently assembled, this collection nevertheless came very near to being lost. Dukes come and dukes go . . . Not all of them appreciate art: Hastings, for example, the twelfth duke, had literally half the manor torn down on the pretext that dry rot was eating away the beams. It was after his death that the Canalettos were discovered stacked cheek by jowl against a wall, while the Sèvres sat on the flagstones of the stables, in a crate with no packing straw.

Today, Woburn is more splendid than ever, thanks to the thirteenth duke and his son, Lord Tavistock. Thirty years of hard work have restored the property's luster. The Canalettos once again hang in the dining room, and in a few months, the Sèvres porcelain will be set out on the Christmas table . . .

Antonio Canaletto

Campo Santa Maria Formosa (detail)
Oil on canvas, 18.5 × 33.9 in.; 47 × 86 cm.

More than in France, more than in Italy, more even than in Venice where he lived and worked, Antonio Canaletto (1697–1768) was loved in England where he became, at an early age, the favorite painter of the British aristocracy, who were drawn to the quasi-spatial construction of his compositions. It was a precision that did not, however, rule out poetry.

25

Antonio Canaletto

*St. Mark's Square
from the Basilica*
Oil on canvas, 18.5 × 33.9 in.;
47 × 86 cm.

Pages 28–29:
The Grand Canal
Oil on canvas, 18.5 × 33.9 in.;
47 × 86 cm.

*The twenty-four "Views" of
Venice that Canaletto painted for
the Duke of Bedford date from
1730. At the time, the artist already enjoyed enormous renown;
after starting out as a theatrical
set painter, he switched to a genre
that was then uncommon: the
urban landscape.*

26

28

Antonio Canaletto

Ascension Day

Oil on canvas, 18.5 × 33.9 in.;
47 × 86 cm.

The paintings in the Bedford
Collection, done in 1730, show how
much Canaletto's style had
evolved since his first works
painted ten years earlier. They
grew increasingly assured and
ever clearer, centering upon a
single, beloved subject: the Sere-
nissima, Venice, whether in her
everyday or, as here, festive dress.

31

Antonio Canaletto

The Grand Canal from Palazzo Bembo (detail)

Oil on canvas, 18.5 × 33.9 in.;
47 × 86 cm.

While the palazzi are festooned with banners and flags celebrating the Doge's boarding of the Bucentaur, while the alleyways swarm with gentlemen masked for Carnival, another Venice, that of the chambermaids and gondoliers, does not escape the fondly perceptive eye of Canaletto, who has given us many wonderfully fresh views.

Pages 34–35:

The Entrance to the Arsenal

Oil on canvas, 18.5 × 33.9 in.;
47 × 86 cm.

In comparison with the capricious Pre-Romanticism of Francesco Guardi, there is in Canaletto a certain naturalism. The Venice he depicts is a dynamic, luminous, active city. This visual accuracy draws Canaletto closer to the Dutch landscape painters, with whom he shared a taste for panoramic views.

Antonio Canaletto

Barges and Gondolas

Oil on canvas, 18.5 × 33.9 in.;
47 × 86 cm.

Fresh from his studio, Canaletto's canvases were loaded onto ships bound for the homes of British lords—the dukes of Buccleuch, Northumberland, Bedford—which, still today, hold the best of eighteenth-century Venetian painting.

37

THE COLLECTION
OF THE INCREDIBLE
MR. FORBES

They warned me. Malcolm Forbes is a man who has everything. A château in Normandy (built by Mansart, of course); a palace in Tangier; houses in London, Tahiti, New Jersey, and Wyoming; a 20,000-acre ranch in Montana; a 175,000-acre hunting preserve in Colorado; a Fijian island (why skimp?); a 130-foot yacht, the Highlander; the Capitalist Tool, a Boeing 727 that flies at a cost of $5,000 per hour; Harley-Davidsons, Maseratis, and Lamborghinis. And a magazine of his own, *Forbes*. Oops! I almost forgot. There's also an extraordinary collection of paintings.

New York, Fifth Avenue. It is nine o'clock on the dot as I pass between the Corinthian columns that flank the entrance of the opulent Forbes Building. Malcolm Forbes' chauffeur-bodyguard meets me in the lobby: "The boss is waiting for you." On the walls of the lobby, the majestic staircase, and the chairman's office (almost as cavernous as Grand Central) are works by Rubens, Gainsborough, Renoir, Gauguin, van Gogh . . . In the corridor is a fleet of miniature ships, another Forbes hobby; behind bullet-proof glass is arrayed a magnificent Fabergé collection.

In shirtsleeves, looking, despite the heat, as cool as a cucumber, Forbes leaps to his feet as soon as I enter his office. I would love to know how, at the age of sixty-eight, he manages to keep in such good shape. With his twinkling eyes behind horn-rimmed glasses and his broad smile, he seems to guess my question: "You see before you a happy man. I enjoy myself as I work. That's why your American colleagues call me the Bob Hope of business. But Bob Hope is no collector . . ."

In the Manhattan building that bears his name (carved in gold letters on the façade), Forbes dashes from floor to floor, showing me his little finds, which bear names like Renoir and van Gogh. On the first floor, his enthusiasm increases a notch; he is especially proud of what he is about to show me.

With good reason. There on the pale green walls, Malcolm has assembled one of the most beautiful private collections of Pre-Raphaelites. They are fashionable today, and thus, expensive. But when Malcolm became interested in them, more than fifteen years ago, he was one of the very first. His friends were more than a little surprised that he preferred the Pre-Raphaelites to Monet or Degas. He smiled: "You'll

The author and Malcolm Forbes in front of his building on New York's Fifth Avenue. It is but a small part of his real estate holdings, which also include a château in Normandy, a palace in Tangier, a ranch in Nevada, an island in Fiji . . . "The only difference between adults and children," declares Forbes, "is the price of their toys."

see, everything I touch turns to gold." Indeed. Today, the least Pre-Raphaelite canvas easily brings $2 million at the great international auctions. And where are the most beautiful to be found? At Malcolm Forbes', to be sure.

If the collection is the work of Malcolm Forbes, the family fortune was begun by his father, a Scottish immigrant who launched his own magazine in 1917. In 1954, Malcolm took over the reins. The results were spectacular; he doubled the circulation in less than ten years, increasing the advertising sevenfold. Today, with a circulation of 700,000, the magazine brings in $8 million a year for Malcolm Forbes, thanks to several marketing coups, most notably the Forbes 400. Since 1982, the annual appearance of the list has been an event. (Think of it: to make the Forbes 400, you need a personal fortune of at least $125 million. To rank with the Gettys, Hunts, Rockefellers, and Malcolm Forbes himself, you need a lot more.) The latest of these coups was the recent announcement that one in five *Forbes* subscribers is a millionaire.

Malcolm Forbes' methods have been unorthodox but effective. The magazine has a forceful, provocative tone. Its specialty is exposing companies from the inside, dissecting the strengths and weaknesses of their executives. And it goes over well with the readers, just like Forbes' editorial, which, issue after issue, swears by free enterprise. To attract advertisers, Malcolm and his editors invite company heads to lunch several times a week. Between the Poulet à la Parisienne and the ice cream, Forbes cites the latest circulation figures and the magazine's importance in the business world. No doubt about it, *Forbes'* best P.R. man is Forbes himself! His message is clear: A C.E.O., if he has any sense or ambition, needs to advertise in *Forbes* magazine. The undecided are likely to be invited on an outing aboard the Highlander, the biggest private yacht at anchor in New York Harbor (the soft sell), or a guided tour of the painting collection (the hard sell).

Malcolm came to collecting rather late; he was well past forty. Like most great American collectors, he turned at first to the French Impressionists, Renoir and Toulouse-Lautrec, van Gogh and Gauguin. And then, during his wanderings through galleries and auction rooms, Forbes happened upon the Pre-Raphaelites, those young English painters of the mid-nineteenth century who drew their inspiration from the poetry of Byron and Keats. He was among the first to recognize the importance of Millais, Rossetti, Ford Maddox Brown, Burne-Jones, and the others over whom all the museums fight today. For next to nothing, he bought paintings that are now worth fifty times what he paid. The result: While a museum like the Musée d'Orsay, for example, can exhibit only two or three mediocre Pre-Raphaelites, the Forbes Collection can boast of more than sixty of their finest works. Not bad for a private collection!

Page 41:
William McTaggart

The Fisherboy

Oil on canvas, 13.4 × 11.4 in.;
34 × 29 cm.

A painter of genre scenes and landscapes, especially seascapes, McTaggart enjoyed great popularity in his native Scotland. Initially very close to the Pre-Raphaelite painters, his style later became freer, as he was drawn to the Impressionists.

Pages 42–43:
George Storey

The Orphanage

Oil on canvas, 40.2 × 60.2 in.;
102 × 153 cm.

After studying mathematics in Paris, Storey decided to go to London to pursue his true love, painting. His first works conformed to the fashion for historic subjects that prevailed in the 1860s. Later, around 1880, he turned (as here) to realistic subjects that are treated with poetry and a very sound knowledge of color.

Pages 44–45:
Winslow Homer

On the Beach

Oil on canvas, 8.3 × 13.8 in.; 21 × 35 cm.

Homer was nearing thirty before he took up painting. After a trip to Paris, his style was initially similar to that of the Impressionists (scenes of country life, beaches, maritime subjects). But in 1881, after a sojourn in England, his paintings grew darker and drew closer in their inner poetry to the work of his British colleagues.

42

John Strudwick

Isabella

Oil on canvas, 39.4 × 22.8 in.;
100 × 58 cm.

The subject is taken from a
poem by Keats in which two
young Florentine merchants kill
Lorenzo, their sister's lover, because they think him too common
for their family. This scene of romantic love serves as a pretext for
the study of a woman's face,
treated in the style of Flemish
and Venetian portraits from the
Renaissance.

Pages 48–49:
Evelyn de Morgan

Flora (whole and detail)

Oil on canvas, 47.2 × 23.6 in.;
120 × 60 cm.

Before a work like this, it is
easy to see why young British
painters like Morgan chose the
term "Pre-Raphaelite" to describe
their opposition to the academicism prevailing in the mid-
nineteenth century; indeed,
Botticelli is Morgan's clear inspiration.

48

James Tissot

The Farewell

Oil on canvas, 33.1 × 20.9 in.;
84 × 53 cm.

Tissot divided his life between Paris and London, where he enjoyed great success and fell madly in love with Kathleen Newton, who was to become the single model for all his paintings (she is the woman we see on the left). When she died in 1882, Tissot chose to leave England; he had just finished this painting, acquired by Forbes in 1970.

THE PRINCE WITH TWELVE HOLBEINS

Despite the bitter cold and the light, icy rain that has fallen across Germany all morning, Prince von Fürstenberg comes out on the steps of the family castle to greet me: "You didn't have too much trouble finding Donaueschingen?" I assure him that in the absence of road signs, giant billboards singing the praises of Fürstenberg Beer have guided us safely through the forest. The idea seems to amuse him: "Naturally! I'm the brewer prince."

With the jolly face of an English officer, lively blue eyes, and a salt-and-pepper mustache, he leads us to the vast salon. Carved oak seats and Flemish tapestries. Servants in dark green and black livery light a fire in the gigantic fireplace. The Prince continues:

"I've had the Kaiser's room made up for you, I hope you'll like it. Kaiser Wilhelm II, of course, a close friend of my grandfather Max Egon."

Splendor and kindness in the heart of the Black Forest. What has brought us here? The most extensive private collection of paintings by German Primitives and fifteenth- and sixteenth-century masters of the Northern school—the acclaimed collection of the Fürstenberg princes.

Extraordinary. No museum, even in Germany, can match the collection assembled here by Joachim von Fürstenberg's ancestors. No other collector can present such an array of works from the Middle Ages and Renaissance.

I will see these masterpieces the following day; this evening, there is more pressing business, a custom that each first-time visitor to Donaueschingen must respect. Here, on the castle grounds, is the source of the Danube. And woe betide her who fails to throw a pfennig in the spring!

Is Prince Joachim superstitious? Terribly. And very much in love with tradition. For generations, his family has collected art and brewed beer. Tomorrow, he will show me with equal pride his paintings and his copper vats.

Saturday morning: A pale winter sun has chased away the rain. In the huge white and gold dining room, where the Fürstenberg standard flies ("or a bordure nebulé argent and azure, the field charged with an eagle gules, beaked and membered azure"), waits a princely breakfast: smoked sausage and country ham, tea and beer. The Prince puts down his *Schwarzwälder Bote* (the Black Forest gazette has excellent coverage of hunting!) and shows me to the castle's large gallery. Carefully aligned

Prince von Fürstenberg at Donaueschingen, his home in the heart of the Black Forest: white and gold paneling, eighteenth-century furniture and multi-hued marble. On the grounds, a second building houses the collection in fifteen rooms devoted to the masterpieces of the Northern schools of the fifteenth and sixteenth centuries.

on the walls are some portraits. "My ancestors. They are the ones who created the collection," Joachim remarks.

He is standing before the portrait presumed to be of Count Unruoch, the founder of the line. Around the year 800, according to the Prince, Unruoch "was one of Charlemagne's most loyal followers!" But his favorite is Heinrich, over there, a little farther along the wall, in his beautiful gold frame: a hook nose, thick lips, a proud expression. Joachim points out a great scar on Heinrich's cheek:

"He received this wound on the Marchfeld, a tremendous battle between Otakar of Bohemia and Rudolf von Hapsburg. It is thanks to Heinrich that Rudolf kept his throne." Joachim smiles at Heinrich; his ancestor fought well.

Since that time, the head of the Fürstenberg family has been Master of the Golden Fleece, passing down from father to son the right to wear the golden ram suspended from a broad red ribbon. Fifteenth, sixteenth, seventeenth centuries. On the walls, the Fürstenberg princes march past, generals and marshals, bishops and cardinals, counselors and confidants to emperors and kings: Friedrich, the schoolmate of Charles V; Karl Egon, the patron prince.

Karl Egon: Joachim has a particular fondness for his great-grandfather, the founder of the fabulous Fürstenberg painting collection. In 1832, he bought a *Procession of Saints* by Hans Schaüfelein, a pupil of Dürer's. The collection, assembled in a matter of years, is dazzling: Grünewald; Cranach; a group of fourteen panels by the Master of Messkirch; the sole retable attributed with certainty to the Master of Sigmaringen; Bernhard Strigel; Barthel Beham. And above all, the *Retable of the Gray Passion* by Hans Holbein the Elder, twelve panels executed in grisaille with colored highlights (whence its strange name) for Kaisheim Abbey—the most beautiful of the works of this exceptional master, active in the twilight of the Middle Ages. A unique collection, which has no equivalent in any museum. (For comparison, the Louvre, with all its riches, possesses not a single work by Holbein the Elder, and the Metropolitan in New York has only one.) If one adds the sculptures and gold and silverwork, it is definitely the most phenomenal collection of fifteenth- and sixteenth-century works still in private hands. "But without the beer, there would be no paintings," concludes Prince Joachim.

In the castle's library—a long room that smells of musty leather—the Prince heads toward a shelf, scales a ladder, and pulls out a manuscript, the letters patent dated 1283 by which Rudolf von Hapsburg granted Heinrich von Fürstenberg permission to brew.

"Later, our most faithful customer was Chancellor Bismarck; take a look at this medical certificate. He managed to get himself a prescription for beer as a rheumatism remedy!"

Today, Baden-Württemberg is not enough for the Fürstenbergs. They export their beer to the rest of Europe and the United States. As a consequence, Prince Joachim is seen more and more often at the big art auctions at Sotheby's and Christie's. I ask him, by the way, if he is interested in the German Primitive painting that is to be auctioned in a few weeks. With a shake of his head, he avoids the question: "You'll see." It's that old Fürstenberg superstition . . .

55

Hans Holbein the Elder

Page 55:

The Judas Kiss (detail)
Wood, 34.6 × 33.9 in.; 88 × 86 cm.

1460? 1465? The exact date of birth of Holbein the Elder is unknown, but it seems almost certain that he was born in Augsburg, where his father was a tanner.

Pages 56–57:
The Judas Kiss
Wood, 34.6 × 33.9 in.; 88 × 86 cm.

Holbein augmented the training he received in his native village by taking a trip to the Netherlands about 1490. There he came under the influence of Roger van der Weyden and received his first commissions, which he executed with a subtle technique in refined colors. His professional success was marred by personal setbacks; sued by his creditors, he fled Augsburg.

Pages 58–59:
Pilate Washing His Hands (detail)
The Deposition (detail)
Wood, 34.6 × 33.9 in.; 88 × 86 cm.

Far from Augsburg, Holbein the Elder carried out, in succession, the three great commissions of his career: the Retable of the Gray Passion *in the Fürstenberg Collection, painted 1498–1500; the* Scenes from the Life of Christ *for Kaisheim Abbey; and* Scenes from the Life of St. Paul, *painted 1503–1504.*

56

58

Hans Holbein the Elder

The Resurrection (details)
Wood, 34.6 × 33.9 in.; 88 × 86 cm.

What is striking in the twelve panels of the Gray Passion *is the contrast between the sober and solemn character of the figure of Christ (inspired by Flemish art) and the anguished, often grotesque violence of the faces of the soldiers and thieves (suggesting a familiarity with the paintings of Hieronymus Bosch).*

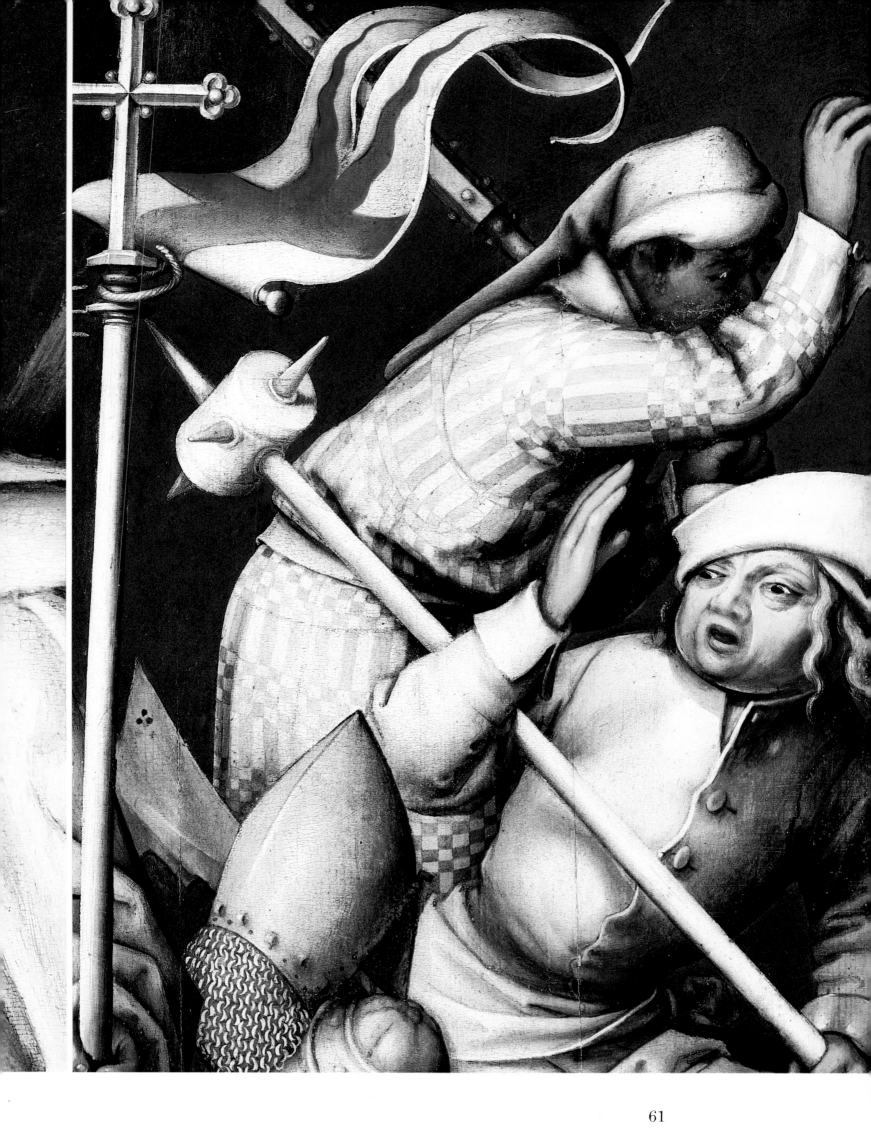

Hans Holbein
the Elder

Jesus Before Caiaphas (detail)
The Flagellation (detail)
Wood, 34.6 × 33.9 in.; 88 × 86 cm.

On the threshold of the Renaissance, Hans Holbein the Elder was the last great German painter who still bore allegiance to the Late Gothic tradition. The whole flavor of his work is here, in this realism tinged with idealism, this continuity infused with novelty.

The panels of the Retable of the Gray Passion *in the* Fürstenberg Collection *reveal another aspect of Holbein the Elder's art: his talent as a portrait painter, in which he felicitously unites insight and elegance. In this way, he conveys the new humanist spirit, the expression of which his son and student, Hans the Younger, would later pursue and perfect.*

62

*The author and tycoon Walter Annenberg in the living
room of his Palm Springs home. Behind them are canvases
by van Gogh and Gauguin, two masters especially well
represented in this spectacular collection of Impressionist
works.*

Walter Annenberg has fond memories of those times: "Beginning in the fifties, I wondered who would be my next 'clients.' It was the era when TV was entering every American living room, so I launched the first magazine devoted to TV programs and what went on behind the scenes."

The success, this time out, is awesome. Circulation grows to an incredible seventeen million copies a week!

It is at about this time that Walter Annenberg starts spending a little less time in his luxurious office and a little more time in auction rooms and galleries. But whether in business or in art collecting, his touch is the same, and his first purchase is a master stroke: a superb van Gogh landscape dating from the painter's finest period, when he was in Arles and Saint-Rémy (1888–1889).

"Thirty-five thousand dollars was a small fortune then," remarks Annenberg, "but I wanted that canvas at any price."

Such enthusiasm could not be satisfied with a single canvas, beautiful as it was. Today, four (yes, four!) other van Goghs have joined the *Landscape with Olive Trees*. When you think that the least square inch painted by van Gogh sells today for millions of dollars, it's clear that Annenberg's quintet is enough to make more than one museum director jealous. The same goes for Cézanne, Gauguin, and Monet. One of Cézanne's most fascinating works, *Montagne Sainte-Victoire*, sits enthroned between a Degas and a Lautrec. Gauguin's most poetic, most original, most accomplished work (*The Siesta*, 1893) is not in a museum, but here, in the Annenberg Collection. And Monet is represented by six of the most celebrated canvases in the history of Impressionism, including an absolute masterpiece, the 1875 *Poppies*. There are paintings in the Annenberg Collection that the Musée d'Orsay, with the world's richest collection of Impressionist paintings, cannot match. But Walter is gracious in victory, declaring that the Orsay has the painting of his dreams, *The Moulin de la Galette* by Renoir. He has consoled himself by buying another Renoir, the magnificent *Portrait of the Daughters of Catulle Mendès . . .*

Pierre-Auguste Renoir

Portrait of the Daughters of Catulle Mendès
Oil on canvas, 63.0 × 50.4 in.; 160 × 128 cm.

After meeting the editor Georges Charpentier in 1876, Renoir was a frequent visitor to his brilliant salon, the gathering place of the political, literary, and artistic luminaries of the day. Renoir became their portraitist, and the portrait that he painted of the daughters of Catulle Mendès, Parnassian poet and writer, no doubt dates from this period.

Claude Monet

The Garden Bench (or Mme. Monet on a Garden Bench)

Oil on canvas, 20.1 × 28.3 in.; 51 × 72 cm.

The years that Monet spent at Argenteuil (1872–1877) are the zenith of Impressionism. All the young artists went there to paint: Manet, Renoir, Alfred Sisley. Like Monet here, they often chose as their subject the painter's garden and the light and shade that played over its magnificent flower beds.

Paul Gauguin

The Siesta

Oil on canvas, 33.9 × 44.5 in.;
86 × 113 cm.

This painting dates from Gauguin's first trip to Tahiti (1891–1893), when he discovered the mysterious splendor of the tropics and, above all, of Tahitian women. Their beauty is marked by a placid strength; their broad shoulders, strong backs, and straight hips suggest a certain asexuality, accentuated by this rear view. They are the subject of some of Gauguin's best paintings, including the Basel Museum's Te Matete and the Annenberg Collection's Siesta, with their luxuriant colors and daring composition.

Auguste Renoir

Reclining Nude

Oil on canvas, 24.4 × 30.7 in.;
62 × 78 cm.

Beginning in 1890, nudes represented an increasing share of Renoir's work. He used only professional models, with the exception of his servant, Gabrielle. The depiction of these women and their pearly skin remains the most appealing aspect of the master's work.

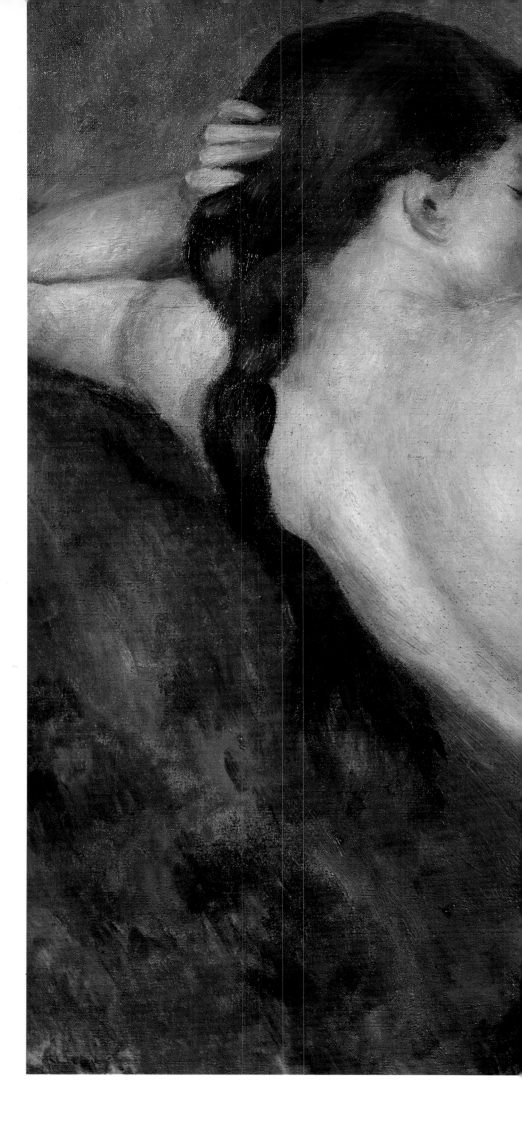

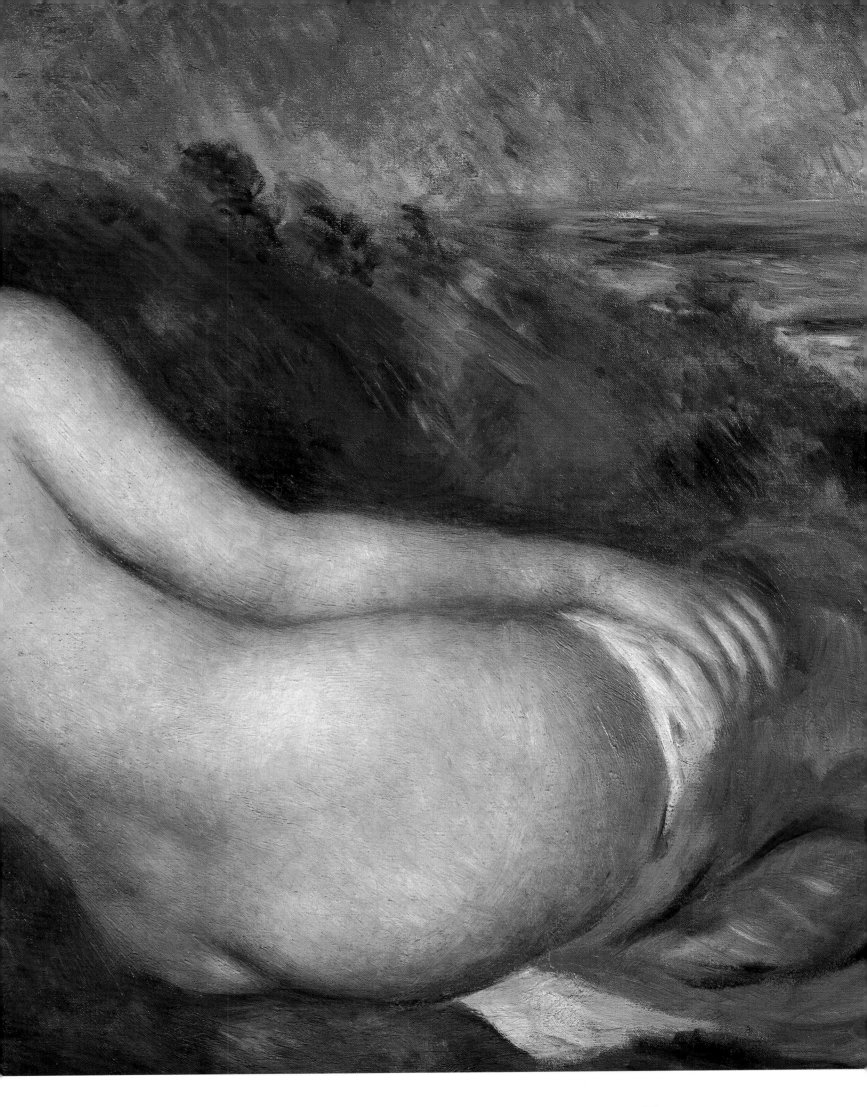

Henri Fantin-Latour

Lilies in a Vase
Oil on canvas, 22.8 × 17.3 in.;
58 × 44 cm.

Initially known for his portraits (especially his group portraits, now assembled in the Musée d'Orsay), Fantin was also a painter of still lifes. They are placed in a bright and subtle light, and rendered with a skill that remains traditional despite the painter's close association with the Impressionists.

Pages 76–77:
Claude Monet

Poppies
Oil on canvas, 20.9 × 28.7 in.;
53 × 73 cm.

Painted near Argenteuil, where Monet settled in 1872, this canvas has become one of the most celebrated of all Impressionist paintings. The work achieves a rarely matched delicacy, without sacrificing the subject's force or freedom. A complete success.

Countess Stephanie's Masterpieces

Behind us, less than forty miles away, is the Austrian capital, "gemütlich" Vienna. But here, in Lower Austria, the Iron Curtain is scarcely more than a few miles away. Ten minutes from Hungary, a little farther from Czechoslovakia, lies one of the most important private collections in Europe, remaining today just as it was almost three centuries ago, when it was created by powerful men in the service of the Hapsburgs—the Harrach counts.

At the mention of the good old days (that is, the Hapsburg reign), Countess Stephanie, who today heads the Harrach clan, barely suppresses a sigh: "The collection that you are about to see is the last private collection in Austria. All the others have disappeared. Been broken up, confiscated, sold."

True, Austria has museums, but no other private collections. The collection of the Princes of Liechtenstein, long kept in their Viennese palace, has permanently returned to Vaduz. Only the Harrach Collection remains.

The history of this collection sounds like a children's counting song. My first was Ferdinand Bonaventure, ambassador to Madrid, who bought Spanish paintings. My second was Aloys Thomas, Viceroy of Naples, who acquired Italian works. My third was Friedrich August, Lord High Chamberlain to Archduchess Maria Elisabeth, who collected Flemish and Dutch masters. And my fourth was Ernst Guido, Grand Equerry of Austria, who was a connoisseur of Neoclassical painting. My whole: four men in the line of the Harrach counts, all high dignitaries at the Hapsburg Court from 1670 to 1780, who were able, by virtue of taste and discernment, to assemble one of the most distinctive art collections that ever was. Famed throughout Europe and threatened, as well. Having barely escaped confiscations and depredations, not to mention the 1944 bombing of Vienna, Austria's last private collection now lies within crossbow range of Eastern Europe.

In 1675, when Ferdinand Bonaventure was Leopold I's ambassador to Spain, the Harrachs had already been in the service of the Hapsburgs for more than a century. They were wealthy, then, but had yet to develop a taste for art. In Madrid, however, Ferdinand Bonaventure found himself in the artistic milieu of Charles II's court, and he experienced a revelation. Bitten by the bug, he called on painters in their

Stephanie, Countess von Harrach zu Rohrau, in the great salon of her castle in Lower Austria. Behind her, the paintings collected by her forebears, high dignitaries in the service of the Hapsburgs and sage collectors who acquired works by Ribera and Carreno de Miranda, Giordano and Solimena, Cavallino and Preti...

studios, patronized the galleries, and quickly made a name for himself in the art market. He purchased not the masters of the past, as was the custom, but works by his artist contemporaries, Spaniards for the most part: Ribera, Carreno de Miranda, Valdés Leal. Little did he know that he was buying some of the greatest names of the golden age of Spain.

With his son Aloys Thomas, the acquisitions picked up speed. Count Aloys thought big; appointed Viceroy of Naples by Emperor Charles VI in 1728, he lived the life of a sovereign-patron of the arts. After reorganizing a financial administration that he found in chaos and initiating a commercial renaissance, he took an interest in fine arts. Lucky for him, Naples was at the time the center of a brilliant school of painting that had conquered first Italy, then Europe, thanks to artists like Giordano and Solimena. They are represented in the Harrach Collection by twelve and eight canvases, respectively. Ambitious works. Masterpieces. And doubtless still the most beautiful group of Italian Baroque paintings in private hands today.

As Governor of the Netherlands, Aloys' son, Friedrich August, usually resided in Brussels. Quite naturally, the paintings he preferred to acquire were Flemish and Dutch, and he did so with panache: van Dyck, Brueghel, Karel Fabritius (the most gifted of Rembrandt's pupils), and Ruisdael. In addition to its Spaniards and Italians, the Harrach Collection became celebrated for the Northern schools—a nice roster.

Like his great-grandfather, Count Ernst Guido was interested in the painters of his own generation rather than their great predecessors. He, too, had a hot hand. Europe, at the time, was living through the Neoclassical revolution, whose leaders were Giovanni Pannini, Pompeo Batoni, and especially Raphaël Mengs. Often paying a small fortune, Ernst Guido acquired landscapes and religious paintings, with the result that Roman art of the mid-eighteenth century is yet another of the strong points of this absolutely amazing collection. It took four men to put it together. It has taken two women, Countess Stephanie and her daughter Johanna, to keep it intact. Their efforts have been well worth it.

Master of the Female Half-Lengths

Three Lady Musicians
Wood, 23.6 × 20.9 in.; 60 × 53 cm.

A masterpiece by a painter who is nameless but certainly Flemish and active about 1530, this small panel portrays three young women musicians. The painted score allows us to identify the ballad—a poem by Clément Marot set to music by Claude de Sermisy—which suggests that these are the daughters of Jean Morel, at whose home the Parisian literary elite gathered during the first half of the sixteenth century.

Pompeo Batoni

Susanna and the Elders (detail)
Oil on canvas, 39.0 × 53.5 in.;
99 × 136 cm.

Installed in Rome, Batoni be-
came the most fashionable Euro-
pean portrait painter of the mid-
eighteenth century. His renown
soon extended to his historical
paintings, which he sent to the
Viennese court, to France, to
Frederick the Great, to Catherine
the Great, and to Count Ernst
Guido Harrach. Dated 1751, this
Susanna remains one of his most
appealing works.

Cornelis Engebrechtsz

Jeremiah at the Well (detail)
Wood, 9.8 × 16.1 in.; 25 × 41 cm.

A strange artist, trained in the tradition of the great masters of the fifteenth century, Engebrechtsz was one of the last representatives of the Late Gothic. His elegant, elongated figures, exquisite palette, and refined, calligraphic style are all evident here.

Pages 86–87:
Jan van Bylert

St. Irene Tending to St. Sebastian (detail)
Oil on canvas, 44.5 × 39.4 in.;
113 × 100 cm.

Bylert, founder of the Caravaggesque movement in the Netherlands, emphasized (as here, about 1630) pure contrasts of light and shade, with the help of a flowing hand that stressed the outline of forms. Thus, his was a very characteristic style that made him one of the best representatives of the Utrecht school.

Cornelis Engebrechtsz

Jeremiah at the Well

Wood, 9.8 × 16.1 in.; 25 × 41 cm.

This estimable painter, whose elegant style sought effects and contrasts of color, marks the end of the Late Gothic era. But the eminence of his workshop, where Aertgen and notably Lucas van Leyden received their training, made the town of Leiden an artistic center that rivaled Anvers and opened the way to the new style, born of the Renaissance. (See detail on pp. 84–85.)

Pages 90–91:

Massimo Stanzione

The Massacre of the Innocents (detail)

Oil on canvas, 50.0 × 60.2 in.; 127 × 253 cm.

A figure in the first rank of Neapolitan painting during the early seventeenth century, Stanzione was an admirer of both the realism of Caravaggio and the classicism of the Carraccis. Out of the fusion of these two was born a style of painting marked by a refined use of color and a great formal elegance that caused Stanzione to be both admired and imitated.

THE COLLECTION OF "LENIN'S AMERICAN"

The "Hammer legend" began in 1921. Revolutionary Russia was being ravaged by typhus and cholera. Far away, in the Bronx, old man Hammer, a staunch Bolshevik, suggested that his son use his college vacation to take over a supply of medicine. Armand set out: London, Berlin, Stettin, Riga, then ninety bumpy hours on a train, seated on wooden benches crawling with vermin. At last Moscow, where he found people dressed in rags and a hotel room without sheets or blankets but with plenty of rats.

Armand Hammer and his medicine were welcomed like the Messiah. The grateful Health Commissioner invited him to accompany a foreign mission to the Urals. "I made the right decision," remarks Hammer. Through the windows of his carriage he looked out on Ekaterinburg, noticing, abandoned on the tracks, trains loaded with ore, emeralds, wood, skins. He proposed a swap: a million tons of U.S. grain for furs and caviar. "That's how I saved the population from famine," he points out. And made a great deal at the same time!

Since then, great deals have followed one after another, with many of them enriching Dr. Hammer's collection of paintings and drawings, including more than a hundred masterpieces. The days of riding in third-class carriages are long gone. Today "Doc" Hammer travels in his private Boeing, with its seats of rust-colored leather and mahogany trim. Up here in the clouds between London and Los Angeles, he tells me how the kid from the Bronx has become one of the most renowned collectors of his day.

"After my first deal, in 1921, I served as a bulldozer to clear the way for exchanges between the United States and the Soviet Union." To prove it, Armand Hammer pushes up the sleeve of his jacket: His watch is a present from Brezhnev, and his cufflinks, a gift from Nixon. But his best memento is from Lenin. . . After the grain exchange, the Russian summoned the American, and urged him to continue, offering him a monopoly on American exports to the U.S.S.R. And, just like that, he added a token of friendship—an asbestos mine in the Urals. A photo of Lenin, whom Hammer describes as "warm and human," still sits on Hammer's desk, ensconced in a beautiful gilt frame. The inscription: "To Comrade Armand Hammer."

Armand Hammer and his Allied Corporation flourished in the East. His Moscow apartment became a sort of unofficial American embassy, the "Brown House," his compatriots called it. Unable to keep up with the work, Armand called his brother Victor, another art lover, to

*Armand Hammer in his Los Angeles office with a Rubens
canvas and photographs of his friends: Lenin and Brezhnev,
Marilyn Monroe and Prince Charles, Nancy and Ronald
Reagan, Gorbachev and John Paul II . . .*

the rescue. It was the beginning of what Hammer calls the "Romanov Treasure Hunt," the beginning of his fabulous collection.

One day, Armand stopped at a modest hotel restaurant in Leningrad. The pirogies were almost inedible, but the plate was what made him choke. A piece of the rarest porcelain, it bore the seal of Nicholas I. The hotelier didn't think much of the china, however; it came from a palace, yes, but it's no good, too breakable! To the delight of the owner, as well as the dishwashers, Hammer traded him some heavy-duty dinnerware for the Czar's dishes.

In similar fashion, Hammer snatched up paintings taken from the homes of princes; diadems; tiaras; icons; silverware; and those marvelous diamond-encrusted Fabergé Easter eggs that were the traditional gifts of the imperial family and the nobility. Armand and Victor also laid their hands on some magnificent pieces belonging to the Czar's collection, such as the crown jewels that they later sold to King Farouk, and the eighteenth-century music box they gave to Franklin Roosevelt for the White House reception room. (One day, it started playing "God Save the Czar" at the very moment that Soviet Ambassador Maxim Litvinov walked through the door!)

With these fabulous collections, the Hammer brothers opened a gallery in New York (where Armand settled in 1931, at the start of the Stalin era). But he kept the most beautiful things for himself—Rembrandts of irreproachable pedigree, authenticated Rubens paintings, first-rate Impressionist works . . .

It is a collection briskly assembled, through spectacular, million-dollar purchases, and will be as easily disposed of. All of it will belong to the United States, with the paintings going to the museum that Hammer is presently building in Los Angeles, and the drawings, to the National Gallery. The man the press calls the "Russian Connection" is truly an American patriot!

Mary Cassatt

Summer (detail)
Oil on canvas, 29.1 × 39.4 in.; 74 × 100 cm.

Closely associated with the Impressionists, American Mary Cassatt pursued her career in France, her adopted country. Borrowing from Renoir the vivid luminosity of flesh and fabrics, and from Degas the truth of the artless gesture, she proved the best woman of the group.

Rembrandt

Juno

Oil on canvas, 50.0 × 48.8 in.;
127 × 124 cm.

Portrait of a Man (Frederick Henry of Orange-Nassau?)

Wood, 32.3 × 28.0 in.; 82 × 71 cm.

Twenty-five years separate these two paintings (dated 1635 and 1660), situated at opposite poles of Rembrandt's career. The panache of the first portraits of the Amsterdam years is succeeded by the splendor of the works of maturity. After 1660, the canvas is illuminated by a singular harmony of form and content.

Francisco de Goya

El Pelele

Oil on canvas, 14.0 × 9.1 in.;
35.5 × 23 cm.

*In 1774, Goya undertook a
series of paintings devoted to
scenes of everyday life that served
as cartoons for a series of tapestries (forty-three of them are preserved in the Prado). These "boce-
tos," in which the landscape plays
a more important role than usual,
are small masterpieces of fluency
and naturalness.*

Pierre-Auguste Renoir

Two Girls Reading

Oil on canvas, 22.0 × 18.5 in.;
56 × 47 cm.

*Approximately contemporane-
ous with the Musée d'Orsay's
Young Girls at the Piano, this
canvas belongs to Renoir's so-
called "iridescent" [nacrée] period (about 1890–1900), with its
amiable style reliant on white
and pink halftones. During this
period, the artist created many
paintings of children, whether
they were the sons and daughters
of wealthy clients or his own boys,
captured in the intimacy of their
daily lives.*

Paul Cézanne

The Siesta

Oil on canvas, 21.5 × 25.8 in.;
54.5 × 65.5 cm.

It is probably Paul, the artist's
son, who posed for this work
painted about 1885. Cézanne was
then moving away from Impressionism in order to "treat nature
by the cylinder and the sphere."
In this, Cézanne's vision presages
Cubism and establishes itself as
the foundation of all pictorial
analysis.

Honoré Daumier

La Parade

Charcoal and wash heightened with
watercolor, 9.4 × 12.6 in.; 24 × 32 cm.

This is the last acquisition of
the four hundred and seventy-
seven Daumier paintings, drawings, lithographs, and sculptures
in the Hammer Collection. It is
also one of the most beautiful,
bought at a Paris auction in 1981
for $213,000. A high price, but jus-
tified. Incisive line, skillful composition, command of color—all of
Daumier's qualities are present
here.

103

Marc Chagall

The Blue Angel

Pastel and gouache, 20.1 × 26.0 in.;
51 × 66 cm.

This work is no doubt related to the series of biblical illustrations commissioned from Chagall by Ambroise Vollard in 1920. Several themes dear to the painter are already present at this date: angels, flowers, and animals, assembled with a spontaneous sense of unreality that will characterize all of Chagall's work.

THE TWENTY TURNERS OF AN EARL

A few miles from the seaside resort of Brighton, the English countryside reasserts itself: arrogantly green lawns, wandering sheep, flowers on parade. And then, suddenly, in this ambience more British than the tea break at a cricket match, a French château. Better yet, a veritable Versailles!

"This is Petworth House, and if you are Madame Prat, Daddy is expecting you," chirrups a voice behind the privet hedge.

Once the initial surprise of this Wonderland is past, everything slowly settles back into place. The architect of Petworth House was mad about the Sun King, and the "Alice" who now slips her little hand in mine to lead me is the eldest daughter of the master of the house, Lord Egremont, second of the name, and seventh Baron Leconfield. She is Jessica, age seven, who continues: "Of course, Daddy has beautiful paintings, but he is also a writer. You must talk to him about it. He'd like that."

"Daddy" is waiting for us on the path to the South Pavilion. Barely thirty-eight years of age, he has one of England's most beautiful private painting collections, including twenty Turners: more than the Metropolitan Museum, more than the Louvre, more than London's National Gallery. Astonishing, but Egremont can explain it: His ancestor, the third earl, was a personal friend of Turner's, and simply acquired the works directly from the painter. Later, when times got hard, the Egremonts turned to farming (cows, sheep, corn, and wheat) to keep up the vast property and preserve the fabulous collection. So it is for good reason that today Max Egremont shows me his fields and his paintings with equal gravity.

A stroll on the Petworth grounds reveals that the wheat fields are magnificent, luxuriant and golden, and the sheep are lovable, as frisky and woolly as can be. But seeing the Turners would be nice, too. Phlegmatic Lord Egremont puts me at ease: It's teatime, let's go back and talk about painting. And art collections.

His collection would not exist without the gentleman in the black frock coat with the dreamy expression whose portrait stares down at us from the library wall: George Wyndham, third Earl of Egremont (1751–1837), adored by women, children, and artists. At least, that's what he said!

The author and Lord Egremont in the music room of Pet-worth House, a pretty château à la Versailles in the middle of the English countryside. Everywhere—in the library, the foyer, the corridors—there are Turners, twenty in all, comprising the most fantastic series of canvases by the master in private hands.

In his life there were many women other than his wife, the sweet Elizabeth, and as a result, lots of little half-brothers and half-sisters making themselves at home on the grounds of Petworth. The vast Egremont fortune allowed the third earl to open his table and home to all: not only had he inherited from his father vast estates in Somerset, Yorkshire, and Northumberland, but his uncle had also left him estates in Ireland. And the numerous guests at Petworth always included artists—painters like Thomas Philipps and James Northcote; sculptors like John Edward Carew. And then there was Joseph Mallord William Turner, who was yet to be recognized as the Protean artist, the painter of genius, that we consider him today. In the first place, there was his off-putting appearance. Always dressed in a rather coarse black outfit and big shoes, he had a hard and impassive expression. In the second place, there was his personality. Timid and gruff, he took his meals while adding barely a word to the general conversation. He was bizarre, to boot. One summer evening, there was a tremendous storm. Immediately, Turner grabbed the first piece of paper that came to hand—a letter—and began scribbling away, recording all the details and effects of the raging elements. Later, Egremont ordered a magnificent fireworks display, just to please him.

The painter had a studio at Petworth and maintained that the huge building particularly inspired him. He stayed there on several occasions between 1802 and 1831, during which time Egremont bought twenty of his canvases. Twenty! This group of paintings has remained intact and is second in number only to the Tate Gallery's collection.

Besides his Turners, the Earl of Egremont had gathered a collection of contemporary English paintings and sculptures that is one of the few collections from the first half of the nineteenth century to survive to the present day. But Egremont also appreciated older works. He had inherited a major collection begun by his ancestor Algernon Percy, the tenth Earl of Northumberland (1602–1668); continued by Algernon Seymour, the seventh Duke of Somerset (1684–1750); and finally added to by Charles Wyndham, the second Earl of Egremont (1710–1763), who bought his paintings while traveling in Italy. The result: not only the score of Turners, but also a collection of van Dykes surpassed only by that of Queen Elizabeth II; a series of splendid works by Reynolds, which would have been worth a story of their own; eight panels by the German Adam Elsheimer, an artist as rare as he is refined; some magnificent landscapes of the Dutch school; and van der Weyden, Titian, Claude Lorrain . . .

The present Lord Egremont has bought nothing, but as he says himself: "I live in a house that has been in my family for eight centuries. The collections have been preserved intact. Those are no small satisfactions."

J.M.W. Turner

Brighton from the Sea (detail)
Oil on canvas, 24.8 × 60.0 in.; 63 × 132 cm.

Why was the Earl of Egremont so taken with this Turner? The man's private life hardly explains the remarkable development of his art. A peculiar existence . . .
When Turner's proud father, a wigmaker by trade, exhibited his son's first works on the shop walls, England had never had any painters. Marvelous portraitists like Reynolds and Gainsborough, yes. But no painters—until Turner set to work.

109

110

J.M.W. Turner

Petworth House from the Lake
Oil on canvas, 16.5 × 24.8 in.;
42 × 63 cm.

Pages 112–113:
Ships at Anchor
Oil on canvas, 23.2 × 35.4 in.;
59 × 90 cm.

   In the beginning, Turner's art
is an art of the solid, the calm,
the mellow. And then, almost im-
perceptibly, there occurs a transi-
tion from the world of classical
painting to the unbridled, turbu-
lent world in which Turner is so
at home. Of course, in the canvases that he showed at the very
respectable Royal Academy,
Turner continued to express his
admiration for the classical cul-
tural heritage. But for himself, he
treated light and color in an unprecedented spirit of abstraction.
As for the subjects, there are few
natural catastrophes that this
genius of sound and fury has not
depicted: storms, tempests, hurri-
canes, fires, avalanches. Wherever
the elements were unleashed,
Turner was watching, fascinated,
feverishly jotting down notes.
"With him," said Egremont,
"sight becomes vision." Precisely.
With Turner, it is no longer a
matter of recreating a place but of
suggesting a simple, luminous
"no-place."

J.M.W. Turner

Hulks

Oil on canvas, 12.6 × 18.9 in.;
32 × 48 cm.

It has often been said that Turner's extraordinary works strongly foreshadow the Impressionists; his sunsets (here seen in a canvas from 1812) anticipate Monet's sunrises. But, unlike the Impressionists, Turner drew only quick sketches from nature, reinterpreting them considerably on the canvas back in the studio and conferring on them the visionary aspect so evident here.

115

The Collection of a Swiss Chocolatier

"As a businessman, he wasn't much good. But he was some terrific collector!"

Andreas Reinhart is speaking of his great-uncle Oskar. The Reinhart name is well known in Winterthur, outside Zurich, which is virtually the private preserve of this family of important industrialists, merchants, and connoisseurs.

"The paintings you will see," Andreas goes on, "were accumulated by my uncle Oskar, patiently, lovingly, during sixty years. The house, the furniture, where the paintings are hung, nothing has been changed since his death in 1965. We haven't touched it. Come and see."

Amazing. The house is a big place on the outskirts of town. Built of stone and slate, it is sturdy and comfortable. Middle class on the outside, but on the inside . . .

Imagine: twenty Daumiers, eleven Delacroixs, nine Courbets, ten Corots, fifteen Renoirs, ten Cézannes. And Degas, Monet, van Gogh, Manet, Picasso. For the Ancients, Cranach, Holbein, Rubens, Rembrandt, Frans Hals, El Greco, Goya, Watteau . . . Who would have believed that this unassuming house was home to such treasures!

The Ali Baba who gathered them, Oskar Reinhart, was solidly built, with a freckled face and red hair (which he lost at an early age), clear eyes, a strong nose, and thin lips. He was a serious and successful businessman until 1924, when he realized business didn't interest him; stock-market prices, cash flow, business lunches—they bored him to tears. What fascinated him was art market prices, the wonderful masterpiece that he tracked down after months of research, the lives of painters that he studied for hours in the silence of his library.

"So," explains Andreas, "at thirty-nine, my uncle ditched everything. It was 1924, and over the next twelve years he succeeded in assembling a world-famous collection. An unprecedented adventure."

Oskar Reinhart was forty years old when he bought his first painting. At that age, others (like Armand Hammer and Norton Simon) had already acquired most of their collections, whereas, until then, Oskar had to content himself with daydreams. And yet, his connoisseurship was precocious.

Little Oskar was as rowdy as the next kid, neither the best student nor the most gifted, but fascinated already by works of art. In

Andreas Reinhart before The House of Cards *by Chardin,
acquired by his great-uncle Oskar Reinhart. Since the connoisseur's death, not a thing has been altered in the family
house, not a painting taken down. This magnificent collection,
which covers half a millennium, has remained intact.*

117

that he was lucky, for Papa Theodore and Mama Lilly lived in a pretty house called Rychenberg, where, at the turn of the century, one might encounter the intelligentsia of arts and letters, including Rainer Maria Rilke and Ferdinand Hodler. Oskar was allowed to sit on a little stool in a corner of the salon and listen to the long conversations during which the art of the Academy clashed with the Impressionist revolution. Reinhart enjoyed a privileged adolescence, until the day when he managed to confess that looking after the family import-export business did not interest him. Well, it was more than Papa Theodore could stand; he told Oskar flat out: If you want to buy works of art, you'll have to earn the money to pay for them. No idlers in the Reinhart family! And so Oskar left for India and Europe, an advance man for his father's firm, Volkart Brüder, which traded in cotton, coffee, and chocolate, and remains today in the hands of his heirs.

Though he obeyed his father, Oskar loved art as much as ever. He took advantage of his years of apprenticeship in London to haunt the British Museum and the National Gallery where he looked at paintings, consulted drawings, studied prints. He followed the same strategy in all the capitals of Europe. In 1919, Theodore died. Soon after, Oskar sold his share of the family business to his four brothers and became "a full-time collector."

He visited auction rooms, museums, exhibitions of engravings, artists' studios, private collections. More and more, the big dealers turned to him when they had an important canvas. Ambroise Vollard showed him a *Montagne Sainte-Victoire* by Cézanne that Reinhart bought on the spot; for the painter from Aix, you couldn't hope for much better! Later Durand-Ruel, the most reliable source for Impressionists, offered him a Monet, the 1881 *Break-Up of the Ice*. The Reinhart Collection was certainly off to a good start: a Nicolas Poussin (a *Holy Family*) bought from Wildenstein, a van Gogh (*Portrait of Augustine Roulin*) from Vollard, a Daumier (*Pierrot Playing the Mandolin*) acquired from Mathiesen, a Renoir (*Sleeping Woman*) from Rosenberg . . . Nice, very nice. And then in 1933, money troubles forced Willem Hansen, a well-known Danish collector, to sell his holdings. Given the importance and quality of the works, the state declared its interest, but hemmed and hawed in the hope of bringing down the price. "Not very sporting of them," thought Reinhart, who made his own offer. And that is how, in one day, he acquired sixteen first-rate Impressionist paintings, including Renoir's *Garden at Fontenay* and a Cézanne *Self-Portrait*. Reinhart's moral: "There are times when even a Swiss German must make up his mind in a hurry." Hurrying seems to have become a habit, for he assembled the bulk of his collection by 1936. After waiting forty years to buy his first painting, he took only a dozen years to acquire a hundred and eighty. Sweet revenge!

Page 119:
Frans Hals

Boy Reading

Oil on canvas, 29.9 × 24.8 in.;
76 × 63 cm.

Few lives are simpler;
Frans Hals painted only
portraits, and the whole
of his long career was
spent in Haarlem.
Even in his first
works, Hals rejected the
Italian style and sought
unflinchingly the most
objective reality. This
appealed to the seven-
teenth-century Dutch
merchant class, who
made him their favorite
painter. But if Hals
aimed no higher than
capturing the likeness of
the sitter, he nevertheless
proclaimed a new free-
dom in his brushstroke
that was very daring for
the time.

Lucas Cranach the Elder

Portraits of Dr. Johannes Cuspinian and His Bride, Anna

Wood, 23.6 × 17.7 in.;
60 × 45 cm.

These two portraits
date from the early years
of the career of Cranach
the Elder, shortly after
the painter settled in
Vienna (Cuspinian mar-
ried Anna Putsch in
1502). Early paintings,
but masterpieces all the
same. The faces, with
their vigorously drawn
features, stand out
against a landscape back-
ground in a harmony
that Cranach would not
always achieve in his
later work.

120

122

Jean-Baptiste Chardin

Basket of Peaches

Oil on canvas, 15.0 × 18.1 in.;
38 × 46 cm.

An intimate little masterpiece, this still life reveals Chardin's best qualities: balanced composition, harmony of color and rejection of trivial detail, which make him an anomaly in the elegant and hedonistic eighteenth century. It was his interest in the "silent life of objects" that Diderot deeply admired.

Pages 124–125:

Édouard Manet

At the Café

Oil on canvas, 30.7 × 33.1 in.;
78 × 84 cm.

The painting depicts a brasserie on the Boulevard Rochechouart, the Cabaret de Reichshoffen, known at the time for its variety show. If the painting's subject is anecdotal, its composition is rigorous and well conceived. The work is one of a series of masterpieces in which Manet extends the expression of visual sensation ever farther.

Pablo Picasso

*Portrait of
Mateu de Soto*

Oil on canvas,
24.0 × 18.1 in.; 61 × 46 cm.

*Painted in October
1901, at the beginning
of Picasso's second stay
in Paris, this work
ushers in the Blue Pe-
riod. Through this por-
trait, whose emotional
intensity is achieved by
the simplification of
volumes and outlines,
Picasso confesses that
van Gogh's influence on
his work was not only
pictorial, but also psy-
chological and moral.*

Henri
de Toulouse-
Lautrec

*The Clownesse
Cha-U-Kao*

Oil on canvas,
29.5 × 21.7 in.; 75 × 55 cm.

*The clownesse
Cha-U-Kao performed
as an acrobat at the
Nouveau Cirque and
the Moulin Rouge.
Lautrec painted her
portrait on two occa-
sions: in 1895, here,
then again in 1896.
After being in the pos-
session of Florence
Gould, the second ver-
sion was put up for sale
in 1985, and created an
auction record of
$5,280,000, making Lau-
trec one of the most ex-
pensive painters in the
world.*

Masterpieces of the Heir to the Kings of Romania

They tell me I'd never have been invited if I weren't a hunter. True to form, Prince von Hohenzollern brought up the subject at the first opportunity: "Yesterday, I was in your beautiful country, in Alsace, hunting." But I am here today, in his beautiful country, to stalk a collection of paintings.

Sigmaringen, a feudal castle, is firmly planted atop a cliff in the mountains of Swabia. In front of the fortified gate waits a square, stocky man, with a receding hairline and a strong jaw: His Highness Friedrich Wilhelm, Prince von Hohenzollern. I attempt a curtsy, he clicks his heels:

"I have had Versailles furniture placed in your room. Of course, the tapestries are from Flanders, and the porcelain, from Saxony, but I hope that the overall effect will please you. Ah! There is also a piano played by Louis-Ferdinand Céline during his exile at Sigmaringen. It is at your disposal."

Protocol and courtesy. Prince Friedrich Wilhelm, an American-style businessman who set up a robotics firm at the forefront of modern technology and flies his own twin-engined plane (every minute counts), is also a connoisseur of the old masters. And in this, his ancestors have spoiled him. Besides the fifteenth-century Flemish tapestries (including an unequaled series by Peter van Aelst), the porcelain from Saxony, and the collection of arms and armor, Prince von Hohenzollern owns the most beautiful collection of Swabian masters in the world. Unrivaled by any museum in Europe or America.

The Hohenzollern dynasty is as powerful today as it was at its founding in 1061. Remarkable, isn't it? Except to the Prince, who explains ingenuously: "My family has managed to keep its domains and possessions intact from its beginnings until now."

So, ten centuries of strength and power for this dynasty, whose first fief was a 2,500-foot hillock in the mountains of southern Germany. Not much to begin with. But, in a few years, this poor rock gave its name—Zollern—to the dynasty, then to the newly built castle, and soon to the surrounding countryside, which was easily subjugated. The proof: A little after 1200, the house had so prospered that it divided. The younger brother's line became the royal and imperial House of Prussia. As for the older brother, Hohenzollern tells the story: "Today I am the

The author and Prince von Hohenzollern in his study at Sigmaringen Castle amidst the mountains of Swabia. The collection of paintings is on display in the castle keep. Elsewhere, Flemish tapestries, German Baroque furniture, and Renaissance gold and silverwork share quarters in this vast feudal edifice.

head of the senior branch. Thanks to their unwavering support for the Counter-Reformation and services rendered to the House of Hapsburg, my forebears, the Catholic counts, were elevated to the rank of Princes of the Empire in 1623."

"Princes" has a nice ring. But the younger branch were kings! Everything was worked out in 1866, when Charles von Hohenzollern was made King of Romania, under the name Carol I. But the best part of the story is that these warriors and wise politicians were also connoisseurs who, generation after generation, accumulated treasures: tapestries, furniture, gold and silverwork, arms and armor. And paintings, remarkable paintings.

The Hohenzollerns began collecting works of art in the fifteenth century: majolica, precious stones, sculptures. But they only began adding paintings in the seventeenth century.

Curiously, it is not German art that the Princes of the Holy Roman Empire were seeking, but the great Italian Baroque paintings, which were then so fashionable among the aristocrats of France, Italy, Spain, and Great Britain. The "reign" of Karl Anton von Hohenzollern (1811–1885) would sweep away all that; although the family fortune, founded upon landholdings and estates, was immense, he decided to sell the whole collection in order to purchase four large panels illustrating the *Story of the Virgin* by the Master of Messkirch (an artist as beautiful as he is rare), two superb works by Bartholomäus Zeitblom, a moving *Crucifixion* by Martin Schongauer. Good picks! The present Prince von Hohenzollern can rest content; works of this quality are virtually unattainable today.

Karl Anton's son followed the same path, making the Hohenzollern Collection the only one in the world capable of presenting such a series of Swabian masters, the masters so sought after now. It is thanks to Leopold and his wife, Antoinette, the Infanta of Spain, both well schooled by their parents, that the collection was enriched by Jörg Stocker's most famous work, the *Retable of Ennetach;* Michaël Wolgemut's *The Annunciation to Mary;* and two works by Hans Schücklin, a founding father of the Swabian school. Two more generations (Princes Wilhelm and Friedrich) built on the work of Karl Anton and Leopold, bringing to fourteen the number of paintings in the collection by the celebrated Master of Sigmaringen. We stand before a pinnacle of painting.

Although the House of Hohenzollern has lost more than a third of its domains since the war, the present prince, Friedrich Wilhelm, has been able to preserve his patrimony while orienting it toward modern enterprises: steel making, robotics, hotels. It all runs smoothly, permitting Prince von Hohenzollern to keep intact a spectacular private collection.

Master of the Thalheimer Altarpiece

Episode from the Legend of Saint Ursula
Wood, 40.6 × 20.5 in.; 103 × 52 cm.

Still anonymous (but placed around 1530), this master is distinguished by his solemn, typically Low-German art, mingled with complex inspirations, sometimes from Westphalia, sometimes from Cologne. In the elegance and suppleness of its forms, his painting reveals a distinct Franco-Flemish influence. There is, in this brilliant colorist, a mixture of realism and sophistication that is completely original.

Jörg Stocker

The Adoration of the Shepherds (detail)

Wood, 80.7 × 58.3 in.; 205 × 148 cm.

Stocker was part of that group of talented artists who each made unique contributions to the German Renaissance. Besides Hans Holbein the Elder, Stocker was certainly one of the first to introduce Italian decorative forms into Germany, while at the same time remaining faithful to the Gothic tradition. This combination is what distinguishes his style.

Pages 134–135:

Master of Sigmaringen

Retable of the Nativity (details)

Wood, 57.1 × 36.2 in.; 145 × 92 cm.

Museums and connoisseurs today search zealously for these masters who made the reputation of the German school of painting before the great stars: Dürer, Holbein, Lucas Cranach. The Master of Sigmaringen (active at the end of the fifteenth and beginning of the sixteenth centuries) is among those who were receptive to Flemish and Italian Renaissance painting, while never repudiating the Late German Gothic.

134

Master of Messkirch

The Adoration of the Magi
(detail)
Wood, 62.6 × 29.5 in.; 159 × 75 cm.

So named because of his principal work, a large retable decorating the parish church of Messkirch, this artist worked in the Lake Constance region between 1520 and 1540. It is there that he met his two principal patrons, the Princes von Fürstenberg and von Hohenzollern. That is why the heirs of these two houses are today, along with the Stuttgart Museum, the principal owners of works by this refined and captivating master.

TREASURES OF THE SHEIKS' CONFIDANT

He has been a collector for over twenty years. Of Renoir and Sisley, van Gogh and Monet, Pissarro and Vlaminck, Bonnard and Picasso. But no one knows him. He rarely attends the great art auctions. Doesn't visit the dealers. Doesn't lend to exhibitions. Doesn't welcome museum curators. Or journalists.

Here I am, however, seated opposite him. Akram Ojjeh—discreet billionaire, secret collector. Yes, he's going to show me his paintings. Yes, for the first time, he will talk about himself. An event.

His childhood, Akram Ojjeh remembers, wasn't exactly a tale from the *Arabian Nights:* His father died when he was eight; his mother became a seamstress to raise him and his three sisters. Hard knocks and hard times. But he at least earned the sympathy of the Lazarite fathers in Beirut, where he got his high school diploma. His uncle had high hopes for him. Since the lad was bright, he'd get a job at the post office. His future was assured, but Akram begged permission to pursue his studies in Paris.

He arrived there in October 1938, at the age of twenty. Two years later, he moved to Nice, becoming a lifeguard at the Hotel Beaurivage. In 1945, recalled to his country, he arrived in Alexandria with twelve trunks of merchandise and "gifts"—luxury goods and a whole stock of lipstick, a commodity unknown in the Middle East. The customs official was an old Lazarite classmate who closed his eyes to the lipstick, putting Akram Ojjeh on the way to his first deal. Today, he can buy anything: airplanes, ships, houses—and some of the most beautiful works in the history of painting.

Above his head, a van Gogh; opposite, a Renoir. They are Akram's two favorite paintings, and that's why he hangs them in his office. He spends more time there than at home. The total effect is opulent: Well-trained waiters in white jackets move about the corridors where bodyguards sporting floral ties and thick black mustaches keep watch. A heavy oak door opens into the conference room. Across the hall lies the chairman's office, decorated with light carpet and dark lacquer, and filled with electronic gadgets. Ojjeh speaks into the intercom:

"No interruptions," he says sharply, then plunges back into his memories.

His big break was meeting the royal family of Saudi Arabia: "One day, Prince Mansur asks me to study the construction of a munitions factory in Jiddah. I tell him that, given the local conditions, the cost of running the operation will be exorbitant. 'Perhaps,' replies the

Akram Ojjeh at home, in his Paris mansion. On the walls,
one of the most beautiful collections of Impressionist and
Fauvist canvases in the world (behind Ojjeh, an astonishing
van Dongen from 1907). It is the first time that the businessman has revealed his collection to the public.

Prince, 'but Saudi hands must learn to work with metal.' That is how I became the first Western businessman to board a plane for Riyadh."

To say that the rest was easy for Ojjeh would be an exaggeration; after establishing himself, he had to avoid plotting from below and disfavor from above. But fortune favored him. In 1971, his mediations produced an accord between the Saudi and French governments on armaments and petroleum products. Ojjeh became the exclusive agent in Arabia for major French companies (Dassault, Thomson, Creusot-Loire), and the material rewards of petrodollars—the painting collection and the Arabian palaces—were the logical consequence.

Riyadh-Paris. Forty thousand feet above the Arabian Desert, Akram Ojjeh is on board his private Boeing, "my magic carpet," he calls it. John, the bartender, pours champagne for Akram's friends with a generous hand (and an experienced one, he was formerly the steward on Queen Elizabeth's plane) while our host has taken refuge from his entourage in his private domain—a large bedroom, a bathroom, a private sitting room.

"My planes, my houses, my cars? They're of no importance, simply tools. But the paintings are another story . . ."

A romance, perhaps. Akram Ojjeh has never concerned himself with the market value of painters. He bought his Monet "because no one had ever painted such a beautiful sunset," his Picasso "because, in this *Mother and Child*, he reveals all the tenderness that he feels for his seven sons and daughters." Surprisingly, Akram owns practically no "Orientalist" paintings; he whose ancestors traveled the length and breadth of the legendary Najd Desert on camelback has become an aficionado of Beaujolais, the baguette, and the beautiful nudes painted by Renoir and Bonnard.

Kees van Dongen

Tango

Oil on canvas, 30.7 × 22.4 in.; 78 × 57 cm.

In 1905, at the Salon d'Automne, a small group of artists, including Matisse, Marquet, Vlaminck, and van Dongen, surprised the public by exhibiting canvases in pure, vivid colors. Shocked, the critics speak of "fauve" (feral) painting. Yet, van Dongen remained loyal for some time to daring harmonies, rapid brushstrokes, and "vulgar" subjects before tempering his style and becoming the sophisticated painter who won celebrity after the war.

Honoré Fragonard

Sketch for "The Lock"
Oil on canvas, 4.7 × 6.7 in.; 12 × 17 cm.

Considered one of the great masters of eighteenth-century Europe and the representative of a certain "French spirit," Fragonard is more than the appealing incarnation of the Rococo style; he expresses with remarkable sensibility the pursuits of the halfcentury of painting that stretches from Louis XV's Versailles to Napoleon's Paris.

Pages 144–145:

Vincent van Gogh

Bridge at Trinquetaille
Oil on canvas, 25.2 × 31.5 in.; 64 × 80 cm.

In 1888, van Gogh departed for Arles in Provence, where he painted his most colorful canvases. The fundamental role that he assigned to color influenced the Expressionists, and later the Fauves at the beginning of the new century.

142

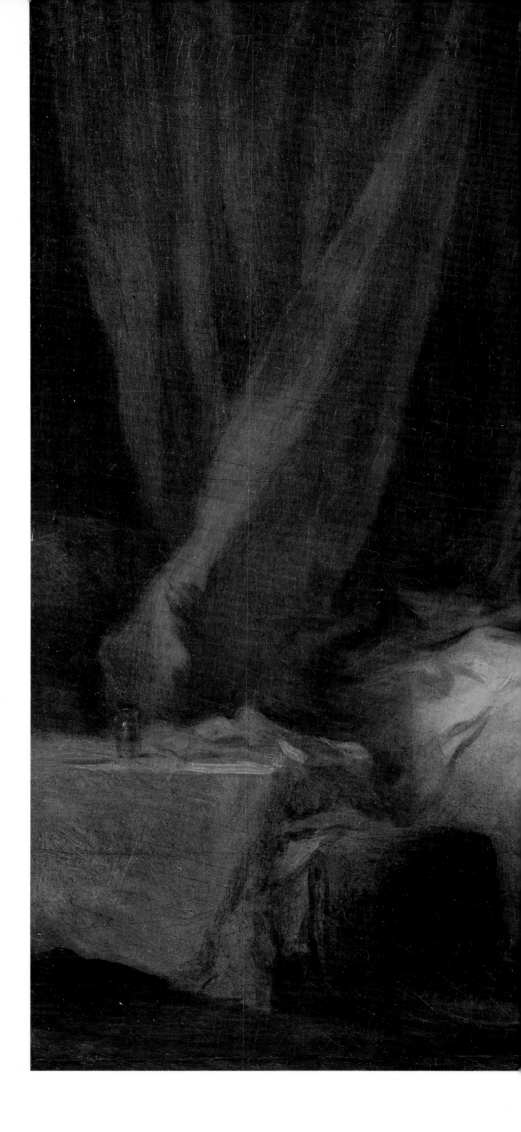

146

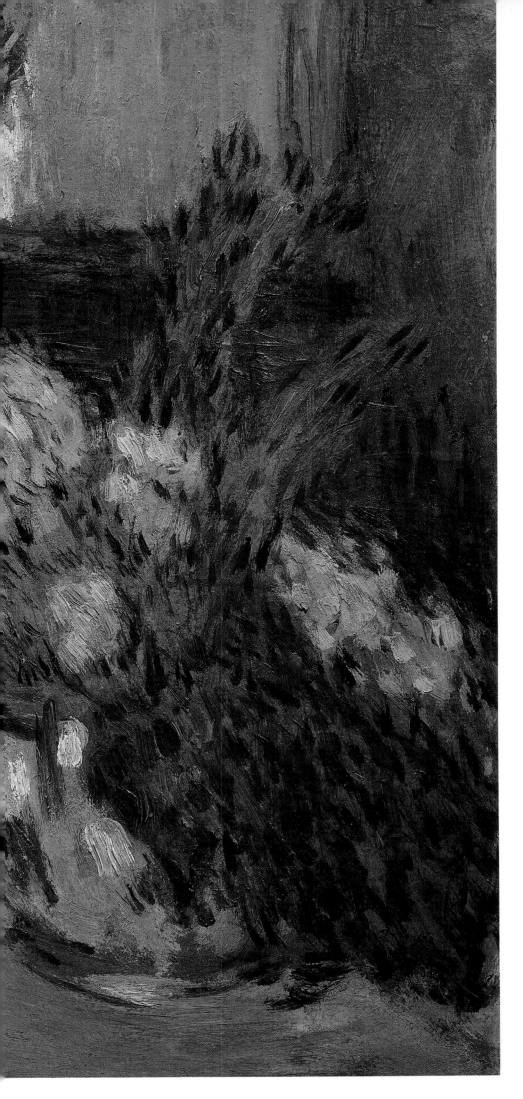

Pablo Picasso

Mother and Child

Oil on canvas, 21.3 × 25.6 in.;
54 × 65 cm.

*In 1904, Picasso settled per-
manently in Paris, where he as-
similated with disconcerting ease
the most diverse influences: Gauguin's colored brushstroke, the
decorative esthetic of the Nabis,
and the sweetness of Eugène Car-
rière, quite visible here.*

147

Auguste Renoir

Bouquet of Flowers
Oil on canvas,
31.9 × 25.6 in.; 81 × 65 cm.

Large Bather
Oil on canvas,
35.8 × 28.0 in.; 91 × 71 cm.

   Two of Renoir's favorite themes: nature and women. The artist's sensuality, already present in his color-saturated landscapes and floral bouquets, has never been better expressed than in the portrayal of these female bodies with their soft flesh and ample forms.

148

The Art of a Zurich Dealer

Zurich's best neighborhood, not far from the lake, is the preserve of the SGPs (Swiss German Protestants). It is peaceful, very peaceful; nothing disturbs the silence. It is clean: Only the occasional fallen leaf trespasses upon the pristine streets. It is well-to-do, but inconspicuous. Thick greenery hides the façades of the multi-storied houses. Just as I place my finger on the bell of No. 7, the door opens on a heavyset, smiling man, with blue eyes behind thin-rimmed spectacles: Peter Nathan. He might be taken for a scientist or mathematician, but the truth is even better. Nathan is one of the great art collectors of his generation, not one of those who spend millions on paintings that then make the headlines, but a connoisseur who has learned about art over the course of years and through countless museum visits.

He is a dealer as well. But not a wheeler-dealer, who buys high, then sells higher. No, Nathan belongs in the company of Durand-Ruel, Ambroise Vollard, and Henry Kahnweiler, the dealers who supported and made known the Impressionists, Cézanne, Picasso and the Cubists. Peter Nathan's discoveries are painters like Chaissac, Estève, and Lapicque, for whom he organizes exhibitions and edits invaluable catalogues, and whose work he encourages. Nathan has a single unbreakable rule: When a painting leaves his gallery to enter his personal collection, it stays put. And while he may be an expansive dealer, he is an unobtrusive collector; his private collection is secret.

Here it is, however. For *Figaro Magazine,* Peter Nathan has made an exception, agreeing to unveil his masterpieces.

"How do you say it? Breeding tells? Is that it?" Aside from the hint of a German accent, that's exactly how you say it. Peter Nathan knows the language and its sayings well. It's true, too, that this saying could be his motto.

1910, Germany: Peter's great-uncle owns a Munich auction house, and business is good. Soon, he has branches in Frankfurt and Berlin. The very conventional great-uncle wants his nephew (Peter's father) to choose a respectable profession, so Fritz becomes a doctor. But how can you resist a calling, and a hereditary one at that! Fritz is more interested in German Romantic painting than the latest influenza. The uncle gives in, and Fritz opens a gallery in Munich. He doesn't forget the lesson. When it is time for his son Peter to choose a profession, he steers him straight to art history. Why waste time on law or medicine when you can spend it with paintings?

Peter Nathan in his large house on the edge of Lake Zurich.
Behind him, symbolically, a canvas by Estève; this collector of
eclectic tastes, in whose home fourteenth-century Italian art
is found side by side with nineteenth-century French painting, also has a passion for contemporary work, which he sup-
ports and makes known.

151

So Fritz and Peter spent their time with paintings, but in Switzerland (the family had left Germany for Zurich in 1936). After detours in New York and Paris, the two "art capitals" where he completed his education, Peter felt that his eye was sharp enough to buy his first painting. The year was 1954.

A rather bittersweet memory: The painting in question is a magnificent symphony in blue, with a little touch of gold on the right; in spite of the title, *Sicilian Landscape,* it borders on abstraction. A glorious Nicolas de Staël. Upon seeing it, Nathan felt his heart beat a little faster and bought it without hesitation, hoping that his father would approve of his purchase. He didn't, and neither did the clients of the Zurich gallery. They stayed away in droves. Did this discourage Peter? Not in the least. For him, the role of the dealer is to perceive before others the artistic talents of the day; those who don't like Nicolas de Staël now will perhaps discover him in ten years, that's all.

Peter Nathan the collector is not very different from Peter Nathan the dealer; they share the same eclectic taste, and for a simple reason. When you search for quality, it is impossible to restrict yourself to one school, or one century. On the walls of the pretty Zurich house, a panel by Bernardo Daddi is perfectly at home next to an abstract composition by Maurice Estève. The fourteenth century side by side with the twentieth. The intervening period is represented by some sublime canvases: Jan Brueghel and Lucas Cranach, Annibale Carracci and Nicolas Poussin, Tiepolo and Guardi, Géricault and Delacroix (when it comes to these two artists, few collections can match the quality of Peter Nathan's), Courbet and Corot, Fernand Léger and Max Ernst ... Peter Nathan has his favorites: Among those he owns are works by Corot, Daumier, and Géricault; among those he will never own are Rembrandt's *Jewish Bride* (in the Rijksmuseum) and Piero della Francesca's *Nativity* (in London's National Gallery). As it is, his collection has a rare style, owing more to taste and knowledge than to money. At a time when works of art are bought for tens of millions of dollars only to be locked away in a safe, Peter Nathan's collection has an old-fashioned charm.

Master of the Schwabach Altar

Christ Leaving the Holy Women
Wood, 58.3 × 46.5 in.; 148 × 118 cm.

This work exhibits an affinity with the "Danube style," which refers to the last phase of Gothic painting in the Austro-Bavarian region between 1500 and 1530. The style is distinguished by a taste for landscape, lively figures and intense colors. Here it is combined with Dürer's influence, which suggests that the Master of the Schwabach Altar had spent some time in Nuremberg.

153

154

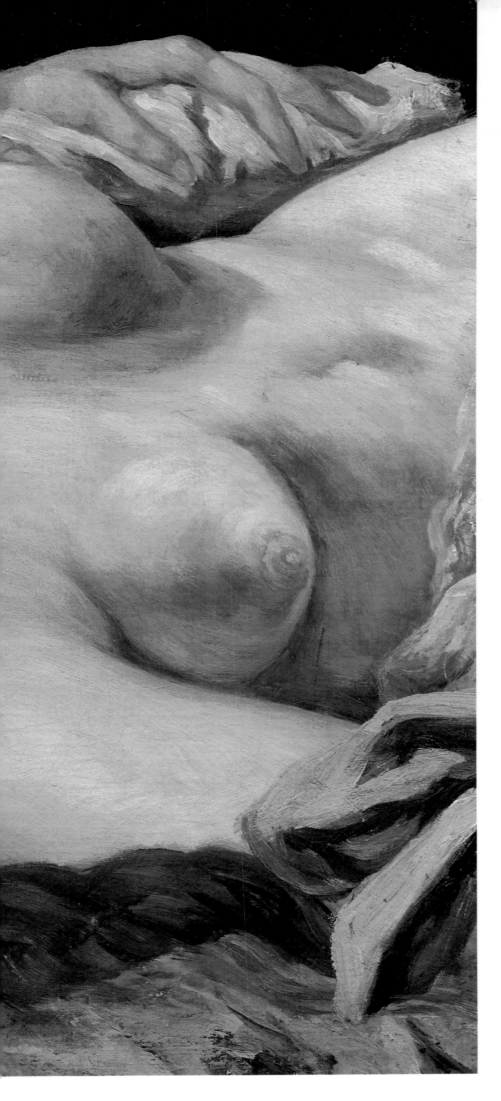

Gustave Courbet

Red-Haired Woman Asleep
Oil on canvas, 22.4 × 31.1 in.;
57 × 79 cm.

Already offended by Courbet's prosaic subjects (Burial at Ornans, Returning from the Fair), the public cried scandal at the sight of his realistic nudes, whose direct sensuality did not, however, exclude poetry and emotion. The richness in the pictorial material remains Courbet's most beautiful quality.

Pages 156–157:

Honoré Daumier

The Third-Class Carriage
Watercolor, 8.3 × 12.6 in.; 21 × 32 cm.

While working for a lithographer, Daumier was hired away by Philipon, the polemicist who founded The Caricature. *Acclaim soon greeted Daumier's prints* (Gargantua, Rue Transnonain), *in which, as here, the line is flowing, the composition dense, the wit biting. Qualities that the Romantics would admire, and the Expressionists remember.*

156

Théodore Géricault

Dapple-Gray Horse
Oil on paper glued to canvas,
18.1 × 13.4 in.; 46 × 34 cm.

 Géricault quickly developed a passion for horses, the principal theme in his work, which are to be found in the military subjects that occupied the artist until 1816. He would later paint several versions of horse races and studies of horses in the stable, in which his palette grew ever more subtle as his concern for form became paramount.

Pages 160–161:
Auguste Renoir

The Watering Place
Oil on canvas, 18.5 × 24.0 in.;
47 × 61 cm.

 Renoir pursued his studies of the figure and landscape simultaneously, applying Impressionist principles to both and employing, as he does here, small curved strokes in place of drawing. As for color, it seems never more refined than during the years 1870–1875.

162

Henri de Toulouse-Lautrec

The Two Friends

Oil on cardboard, 17.9 × 26.6 in.;
45.5 × 67.5 cm.

The admiration that he had for Degas prompted Lautrec to choose, like him, "modern" subjects. He transfigured bars, circuses, honky-tonks, and brothels by means of a curious lyricism fashioned out of shimmering colors and compositional artifices. He was above all a remarkable draftsman, with a sharp, bold, expressive line.

A New York
Architect with
a Passion
for Drawings

N
ew York at summer's end—glorious days when the scent of
flowers floats in the air and golden dust floats in the light. I
go into raptures, but Ian Woodner abruptly cuts me off: "This
light flattens forms, drowns the lines. There's nothing worse."
Tall, with the look of a condottiere and a trim mustache, Ian
Woodner, at the age of eighty-five, has lost none of his fire. His disgust
is understandable: He builds skyscrapers and buys works of art. The
skyscrapers should be seen in the harsh, metallic New York light, when
they stand out against the sky, not when a steamy haze blurs the sky-
line. As for the works of art, they are drawings, certainly among the
most beautiful in the world, but vulnerable to changes of temperature
and humidity. They don't like the heat either.

Skyscrapers and drawings, a singular combination. Ian
Woodner is ever the pioneer, ever the first. He began building the skyscrapers over sixty years ago, during the heroic era of skyscrapers. And
he began to collect the drawings thirty years ago, before these precious
sheets of paper became fashionable. Today, they are hunted down by collectors to the point where they are often more expensive than paintings.
As a result, Ian Woodner is now a very rich man, and the owner of the
most beautiful private collection of drawings in the world: Fra Angelico
and Botticelli, Raphael and Cellini, Brueghel and Dürer, Cranach and
Holbein, Matisse and Picasso . . . All told, five hundred masterpieces that
any museum would envy. But first, what a story!

When Ian Woodner came into the world, in 1903, in a poor
New York neighborhood, his Polish parents were among the thousands
of immigrants come to try their luck in America. If their life wasn't
exactly poverty, it wasn't the lap of luxury either: His mother worked;
his five brothers and sisters, too; only Ian went on to college. He was
certainly gifted, winning diplomas, degrees, and doctorates at a precocious age and with honors. He became the youngest architect of his
generation.

Ian Woodner in the living room of his New York apartment.
Because of their vulnerability to light, he keeps the five
hundred drawings of his fabulous collection not on the walls,
but in special portfolios. For us, however, Woodner has agreed
to take out his Fra Angelicos, Botticellis, Raphaels, Cellinis,
Dürers, Rembrandts, Watteaus, Goyas . . .

The year was 1925, and it was an exciting time—the golden age of the skyscraper. Daring was called for; everything was possible. In the domain of city planning, as in that of housing, Woodner innovated, imagining solutions that were both beautiful and practical (much like his contemporary, Le Corbusier). No wonder that Woodner's firm soon became established in New York and in Washington, D.C. His poor childhood was merely a memory.

Then Woodner realized that he loved not only architectural drawings but artists' drawings as well. He remembers what it was like:

"I can tell you that after World War II you had to be pretty eccentric to be interested in drawings. There were connoisseurs of painting, all ready to pay a lot of money, but not for drawings. *They* were sold in lots of eight or ten, and nobody gave a darn."

Woodner, however, did give a darn, all the more so because beautiful sheets could be had for little. One after the other, he bought a *Peasant Playing the Bagpipes,* which later turned out to be one of the rare known drawings by Brueghel the Elder; a biblical scene (*The Tax-Collector and the Pharisee*) in which today we see one of the New Testament subjects that most inspired Rembrandt; or some drawing depicting a naked man. That was quite a story . . .

1959: The dealer offering the drawing to Woodner asks for $18,500. "Why so much?" gasps Woodner. Yet before the dealer replies, he has decided to buy.

It must have been his lucky day. Drawn by the great Benvenuto Cellini, the naked man is a study of a satyr planned for the Porte Dorée at Fontainebleau—a splendor, certainly the most famous drawing in the world. And which, if it were put up for sale today, would bring at least a hundred times the price Woodner paid for it . . .

For Woodner is no longer the only person with a passion for drawings. In recent years, to enrich his collection, he has had to spend enormous sums: $4.4 million, for example, in July 1984 for a work by Filippino Lippi. Such a price would have been unthinkable ten years ago, but Woodner remains philosophical: "The feeling that a drawing inspires can make you forget the price. I still come out ahead."

Lucas Cranach

Portrait of Christian II of Denmark
Watercolor, 12.2 × 9.1 in.; 31 × 23 cm.

We know little of Cranach's early career. In 1504, Frederick the Wise summoned him to Wittenberg, where he lived for almost fifty years as Court Painter in the service of the three Electors. His position did not prevent him from carrying out commissions for other notables of his time, such as the King of Denmark or Martin Luther.

167

Hans Hoffmann

Squirrel

Watercolor, 9.8 × 7.1 in.; 25 × 18 cm.

Active in Nuremberg and Prague, where he was in Rudolf II's personal service from 1585, Hoffmann became known for his portraits and especially his drawings of animals in which, following Dürer, he married sharp observation with a sense of poetry.

169

170

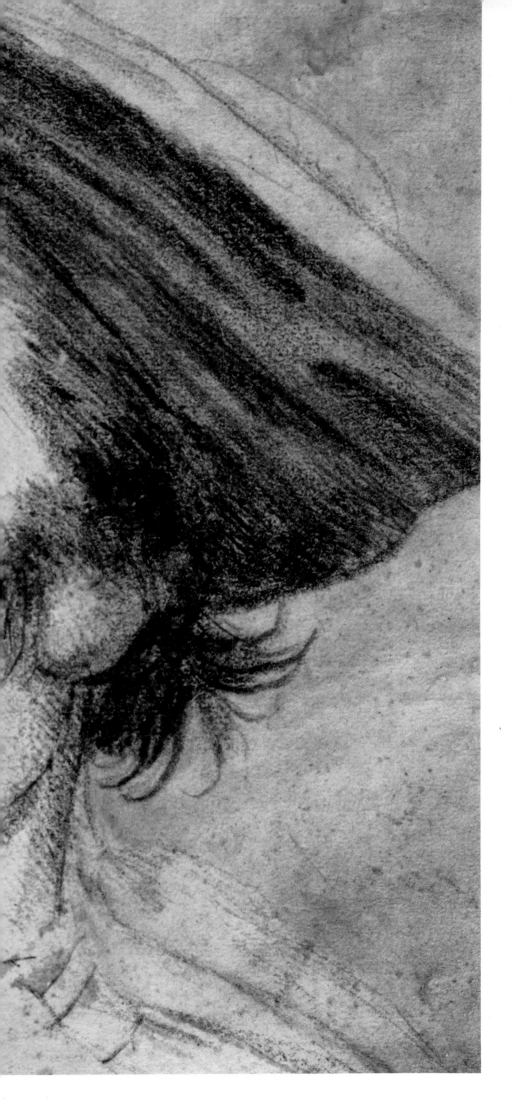

Holbein the Younger

Portrait of a Young Man
Black and red chalk, 11.8 × 7.5 in.;
30 × 19 cm.

A precocious genius, Holbein the Younger saw his renown as a portrait painter spread rapidly, first to Basel, then to London, where the artist settled permanently in 1532. Having entered the service of Henry VIII, he produced a series of likenesses of the King and his court that combine, in a synthesis unique at the beginning of the sixteenth century, the Gothic tradition and the humanist Renaissance.

Albrecht Dürer

Wing of a Blue Jay

Watercolor on vellum, 7.1 × 9.4 in.;
18 × 24 cm.

*The first watercolors of
Dürer's career appeared when
the artist visited Venice, in
1494. At the same time as his
interest was awakened to the
new theories of the Italian Renaissance, he showed a parallel
curiosity for things of nature,
which he observed with a realism typical of the Northern
schools. It was a stimulating
mixture that gave birth to some
of the great masterpieces of the
graphic arts: the Louvre's* View
of the Arco Valley, *the* Blue
Crow *in Vienna's Albertina,
the British Museum's* Pond in
the Forest, *or Woodner's own*
Wing of a Blue Jay.

173

Odilon Redon

The Cactus Man

Charcoal, 17.7 × 11.8 in.; 45 × 30 cm.

Although a contemporary of the Impressionists, Redon pursued his investigations at a distance from the movements of the day. His work, at the frontier between the vague and the ambiguous, places him in the company of the great visionaries, from Goya to Moreau. Long misunderstood, Redon is today considered one of the richest and most complex figures of the nineteenth century, and the precursor of the Symbolist movement.

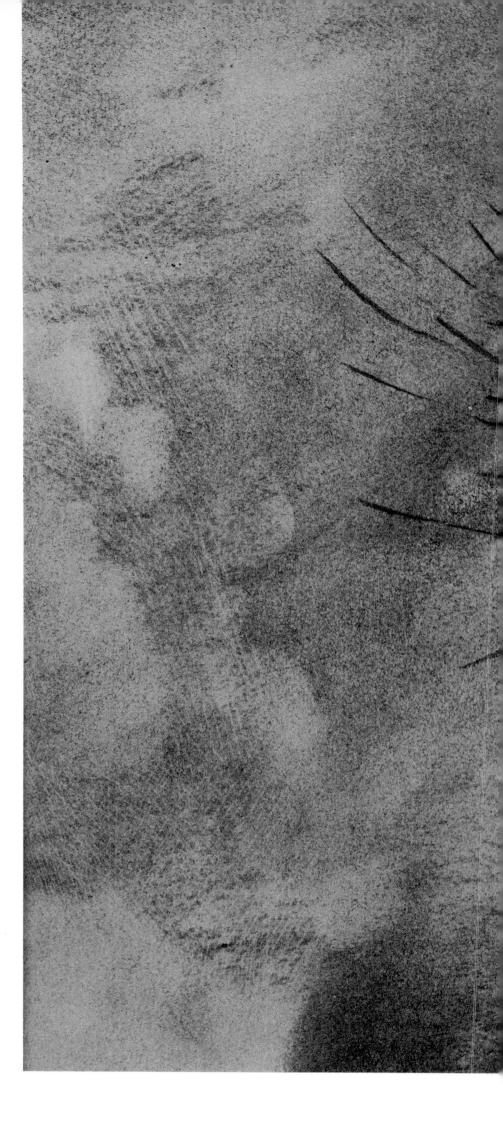

A Samurai Industrialist Pursues Western Painting

"Do not forget to take off your shoes, kudasai. . ." My shod feet on the tatami were inexcusable. "Like putting water in Château-Lafite 1978," Kenichiro Oohara graciously explained. I contemplated the gravity of my crime and entered barefoot the Ooharas' big, traditional wooden house, built during the eighteenth century and one of the oldest in Japan. The present head of the family, Kenichiro—our connoisseur of Château-Lafite—has inherited one of the two most important collections of Western art in Japan. That is the reason for my trip to Kurashiki, some four hundred miles from Tokyo on the southeast coast of Honshu.

This village, where one is suddenly thrust several centuries back in time, is the cradle of the Oohara family and the home also of their magnificent collection. The industrial smog and development that plague Japan have spared Kurashiki. Grand residences dating back to the Tokugawa and Meiji eras border the canals that give the town its unusual architecture of bridges and steps. Elsewhere, magnificent wooden warehouses serve as a reminder that the town was the center of great commercial activity during the Shogun era. It is from cotton, grown in the fertile soil of Kurashiki, that the Oohara fortune was born.

During the Meiji era, industrialization swelled the family business to national scale. Today, "Kuraray" is worldwide, synonymous with the textile industry, and still in the hands of the Ooharas. But the best part is that, from the beginning, this family of industrialists was taken with art and music; the Oohara Collection, which continues to grow, was begun almost a century ago.

It started with the grandfather, Magosaburo, who was twenty years old in 1900, but no kid. In a few years, he doubled the size of the family textile mills. Silk was very nice, of course, but also very expensive. So he introduced Japan to rayon, swathing the country in it from Hokkaido to Kyushu. That is how the Oohara fortune was built; beginning with simple cotton spinning, each generation has managed to be at the forefront of textile progress. If Japan no longer buys nylon from Amer-

The author and Kenichiro Oohara in front of the Oohara family home in Kurashiki, a pretty village on the southeast coast of Honshu that has preserved its historic character. The interior of the house remains traditional, with few works of art on display. The collection of Western paintings is housed in an adjoining building, designed in Neoclassical style.

177

ica, it is because the Ooharas have invented Vinylon: just as good, but cheaper! The same goes for Clarino, a synthetic leather. Recently, they have moved into textile-derived chemicals, and with as much success as ever.

His money quickly earned and well deserved, grandfather Magosaburo used it to buy Impressionist paintings. And that, in 1920 Japan, was revolutionary. When Oohara's first Monet arrived in the Land of the Rising Sun, contemporary Western painting was completely unknown. Monet? They'd never heard of him. Oohara was a pioneer. If today the Japanese are the principal buyers at the great international art sales (remember the $39 million Yasuda, an insurance company, paid for van Gogh's *Sunflowers*), it is because more than half a century ago, Oohara the textile manufacturer was captivated by *Water Lilies* . . .

Oohara had the assistance of his childhood friend Torajiro Kojima, an astonishing character. Kojima grew up to be a painter. He went to Europe, where he met Monet, Matisse, Marquet, and the whole gang. He communicated his enthusiasm to Oohara, who sent him back to Europe, his pockets bulging, with instructions to buy the best the Paris market had to offer. And so it was that Manet's *Portrait of a Woman,* Renoir's *Bather,* Degas's *Dancers,* and Toulouse-Lautrec's *Portrait of Marthe X* set off for Japan. As for Monet's *Haystacks* and Matisse's *Portrait of the Artist's Daughter,* Kojima brought them straight from his friends' studios—what better provenance! In all, Kojima bought more than twenty-five paintings for Oohara during the single year 1920. The collection was off to a terrific start . . .

Magosaburo's son, Soichiro, shared his father's passion: the Cézanne, the Gauguin, the Sisley are his acquisitions. But this lover of tradition was also an avant-gardist. He enriched the collection with twentieth-century works, including Matisse, Picasso, Braque, Rouault, and a few dabblings in abstract art, such as Wassily Kandinsky's masterpiece *Points,* acquired as early as 1949. A daring purchase!

Today Soichiro's son, Kenichiro, a small dynamic samurai, manages the textile business and the art collection with equal good humor. He admits that his tastes tend more toward the American lyric painters Jackson Pollock and Sam Francis (both represented in the collection). But there is, after all, a family tradition to uphold; if a beautiful Impressionist painting appears on the market, then in memory of his ancestors, Kenichiro will try to acquire it. Especially if it's a van Gogh, the single Impressionist missing from this superb collection!

El Greco

The Annunciation (detail)

Oil on canvas, 42.5 × 31.1 in.; 108 × 79 cm.

Nourished by his Cretan heritage (the painter was born in Candia, capital of what was then a Venetian possession), together with the lessons of the Italian Renaissance and the atmosphere of Toledo, El Greco's imagination adheres to the prescriptions set forth by the Council of Trent. Whence the artist's frequently repeated themes, such as this Annunciation, *painted about 1575.*

Imagination (details)
Oil on canvas, 103.9 × 58.3 in.
264 × 148 cm.

The creator of immense series for the museums of Amiens, Marseilles, and Lyons, for the Sorbonne and the Pantheon, Puvis de Chavannes was the most prolific muralist of the late nineteenth century. His taste for spare lines, softened colors and balanced compositions has captivated painters as distant from academicism as Gauguin and Picasso.

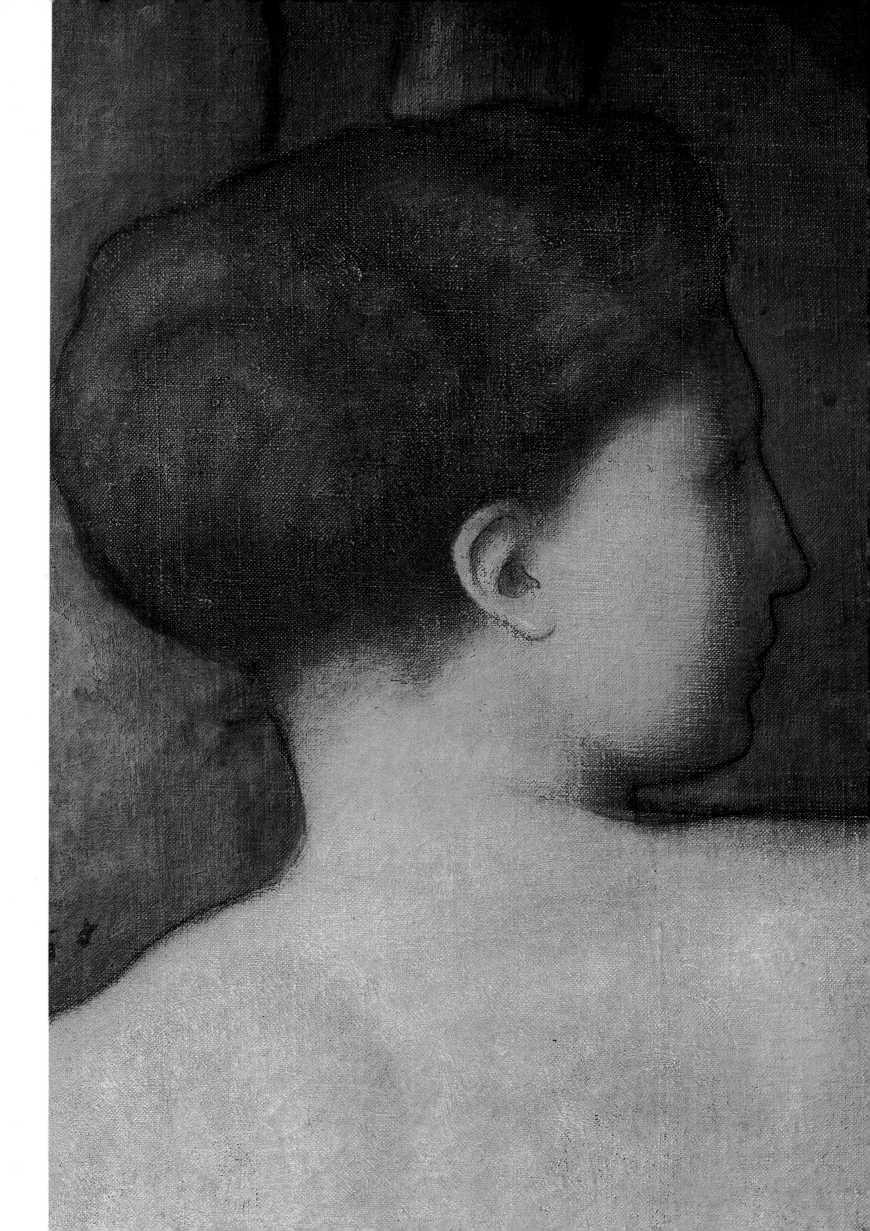

Giovanni Segantini

Afternoon in the Alps

Oil on canvas, 33.5 × 31.1 in.;
85 × 79 cm.

*Alpine landscapes remained
the favorite motif of Segantini,
whose naturalism is attentive to
effects of light. A brilliant coloris
and a skillful draftsman, the artist enjoyed a certain celebrity
during his lifetime (1858–1899).
Today, the bulk of his work re-
sides in a St. Moritz museum
dedicated to the artist.*

182

Henri de Toulouse-Lautrec

Portrait of Madame Marthe X
Oil on canvas, 35.0 × 31.5 in.;
89 × 80 cm.

Greatly influenced by Degas's art, Toulouse-Lautrec sought bold compositions. Another influence—Japanese woodcuts—is evident in the arbitrary division of the canvas and the large, dynamic voids. Such qualities explain the presence of this beautiful portrait in the Oohara Collection.

Pages 186–187:
Claude Monet

Haystacks
Oil on canvas, 26.0 × 31.9 in.;
66 × 81 cm.

Monet, who had been living at Giverny for seven years, purchased a house in 1890. It was at that time that he exhibited his great series devoted to single subjects: Poplars, Rouen Cathedral, Water Lilies, *and* Haystacks, *which are all so many investigations of "instantaneity." Prized by connoisseurs and museums, these canvases are today the most sought after of Monet's works.*

Gustave Moreau

The Song of Songs (detail)
Oil on canvas, 14.6 × 7.5 in.; 37 × 19 cm.

Gustave Moreau's elegance and his fondness for ornamentation fascinated the Symbolist poets Stéphane Mallarmé and Henri de Régnier, and also attracted André Breton and the Surrealists. All of them saw in Moreau's refined chromatic effects and his subjects drawn from Greek and Eastern mythology the delicious charm of fin-de-siècle estheticism.

189

Photographic Credits